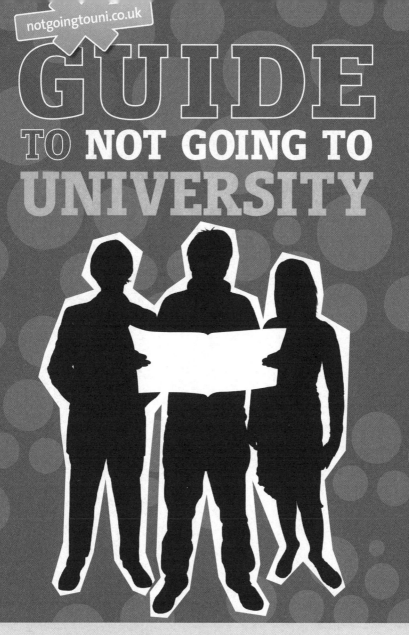

notgoingtouni.co.uk

GUIDE
TO **NOT GOING TO**
UNIVERSITY

ANDREW SHANAHAN

PEARSON

Harlow, England • London • New York • Boston • San Francisco • Toronto • Sydney
Auckland • Singapore • Hong Kong • Tokyo • Seoul • Tai~~~
Cape Town • São Paulo • Mexico City • Madrid • Amsterda~

D0315459

CONTENTS

FOREWORD

Peter Jones, CBE

Founder of the Peter Jones Enterprise Academy (www.pjea.org)

Deciding which career path to take is undoubtedly daunting. After all, there are lots of different options and a seemingly endless list of questions to consider.

Should I get out into the world of work? What about the recession?

Should I continue studying? But what about vocational qualifications?

The key to making good decisions about your career is much the same as making good decisions in the world of business; arm yourself with as much information as possible and really try and understand what's happening in the marketplace ... at the same time as understanding your own USPs (Unique Selling Points) and your passions.

And that's where this easy-to-read book can help, by providing you with the insights and information you need to make the best possible decisions so you get on the career path that's right for you.

Whatever you do, don't panic, no matter what grades you achieve ... the reality is that there are lots of different routes and options to moving forward on your personal career journey and, in my opinion, this book can definitely help you.

Good luck.

FOREWORD

Chris Jones

Director General, City & Guilds

At City & Guilds, our purpose is to enable people and organisations to develop their skills for personal and economic growth. As the UK's leading vocational education organisation, we offer over 500 qualifications across 28 industries and every year we help approximately two million people start their learning journey.

Vocational qualifications open up so many doors and opportunities in a variety of sectors, providing people with the key skills they need to succeed. It's not just us that think this – employers are increasingly viewing skilled individuals as integral to business growth.

Whether you're interested in plumbing or photography; construction or care; floristry or food, a City & Guilds qualification can place you on the right path to employment. And you'll be in good company; household names such as Stella McCartney, Jamie Oliver, Alan Titchmarsh and Karen Millen all kick-started their careers with City & Guilds.

I hope this guide gives you an insight into just some of the options available to you through the vocational route. City & Guilds firmly believes that learning has no limits, and we want to help people of all ages discover their talent and unlock their potential.

INTRODUCTION

This Book In 60 Seconds

"You can do anything you want to do."

Did anyone ever tell you that? Maybe a parent, an inspirational teacher or close friend? They were lying. That's the only logical conclusion that young people who are on the verge of leaving school or college can possibly come to. How on earth are you supposed to be free to choose any path you like when so many different resources have failed you in explaining precisely what you can do and how to do it?

If they were being honest that supposedly inspirational sentence would more likely have sounded like:

"You can do anything you want to do, providing it's going to university or something that I've heard of."

Consider this statistic from City & Guilds: 75 per cent of school leavers were aware of university options, only 46 per cent were made aware of apprenticeships. So, less than half of the people making a decision about what to do for the rest of their lives have any idea about the merits of apprenticeships. We can probably assume then that if they're poorly informed about a major route like apprenticeships then they are equally uninformed about foundation degrees, sponsored degrees, vocational qualifications, employer programmes, gap years, starting their own business or getting a job.

No one is saying that going to university is a bad idea. University graduates earn on average 85 per cent more than people who leave with only GCSEs. But university is not without risks. Thanks to tuition fee rises, going to university could leave you with debts of over £50,000. Currently one in ten graduates leaves university and does not find a job. At all. 40 per cent of university-leavers will not be in a graduate-level job, six months after they've thrown their pointy hat in the air. The worst paid 15 per cent of graduates earn less than the average for those with only GCSEs. Dropout rates for university are as high as 28 per cent.

The evidence is overwhelming. If you are making the choice to go to university it has to be with a full understanding of the risks. We believe it also has to be a choice you make having understood the full range of alternatives and other routes to qualifications, including weird-sounding options like being paid to get a degree.

This book is about your future. It's been put together because at this time young people are under attack. The financial problems that the world is in have been proven to hit the younger generations harder than any other element of society. Youth unemployment is at a historically high level and the media has decided to demonise an entire generation as hoodie-wearing thugs.

Despite this we are excited about your future. We believe that you are at an incredibly challenging moment in your life. It can be terrifying to leave school or college and take the next step, but it can also be exhilarating. The amazing thing is that there are so many options available to you that, judging by the statistic above, you won't know anything about. If you're wondering what this book will give you we can sum it up in a sentence:

"You can do anything you want to do."

Who are we and why do we want to help?

Good question. We're Not Going To Uni – the UK's leading provider of 360 degree careers advice. That means that we look at every path students can take when they leave school and investigate them all equally.

Although we're called Not Going To Uni, don't make the mistake of thinking that we're somehow anti-university. We love universities, students, graduates and lecturers – but we think that the current generation of school-leavers are put under too much pressure to pick university as their next step.

What you will get from reading this book is three things. First, a clear route to help you research your next step and decide what you want to do. Second, you will get exposure to all of the various paths that you can take to reach your goal. Finally, we'll share some of the secret shortcuts that exist when you're looking to get ahead in life. We really do believe you can do anything you want to do, but the first step in doing that is to get the clearest idea possible of all the things that you can do.

PR . . .
. . . Performance Rocks

we pray for Japan

Lady Gaga drank one cup of tea and raised $75,000 for victims of the Japanese Tsunami

The Power of PR in Action

Could you handle it?

PR Higher Apprenticeships

Do you have the drive and ability to change how people view the world and want to learn the skills in a proper working environment? To find out more - visit:

  @PRApprentices PR Apprenticeships

www.prapprenticeships.com

Apprenticeships   cfa   prca   PEARSON   edexcel

'I DON'T KNOW WHAT I WANT TO DO'

This chapter in brief

- Lack of preparation leads to a feeling of not knowing what to do with your life, which in turn leads to frustration.

- Bad life-wasting decisions come from not addressing that frustration.

- To remove the frustration and find out what you want to do there are three stages: research; trial and error; action.

- The research phase contains just three steps: understanding yourself; removing negative influences; creating a longlist.

- This chapter guides you through the research phase and helps you deal with the frustration.

- A short rant about the importance of life, death and the Rector of the University of St Andrews.

It's wonderful to have a tantrum. In many ways it's crazy that we teach children that they're a bad thing. After all, a tantrum is just a physical (and audible) way of expressing the sheer frustration that we sometimes feel in life. How on earth are you supposed to choose what you want to do for the rest of your life? TANTRUM! We can put someone into space but no one can invent a biscuit that makes you lose weight? TANTRUM! Why do I have to get up on cold mornings and leave the house? TANTRUM!

For the purposes of career frustration tantrums are fine; having a good shout and a scream and throwing yourself to the floor (we are legally obliged to tell you that you have to do this carefully) is perfectly acceptable. However, it's only acceptable if you then pick yourself up, apologise for scaring the cat, take a deep breath and work out how you're going to get past the frustration.

Let's take the example of not knowing what you want to do for the rest of your life. It is so frustrating when you're not sure where you're going and all of the answers and paths seem to be hidden. Wouldn't it just be easier if someone told us what we wanted to do? Well, yes. In many cases school leavers do believe the first person who comes along and tells them what they should be, whether it's a parent or a careers advisor. Unfortunately, it's rarely actually a good match for who we are as a person and what we want to do. So, we'll allow you to have one last 'I don't know what I want to do with my life' tantrum and then we'll get on with solving the initial issue. Ready? Off you go.

Better? Good. Deep breath and let's begin.

The first thing to understand is that all the times you've been shouting out that phrase, you never had it quite right. You see the full sentence should be, 'I don't know what I want to do with my life, but how amazing that I'm going to get the opportunity to find out!' Every time you find yourself getting annoyed with the decision making to come you have to remind yourself that although it can feel like a huge weight on you, that's because for the first time you've got some responsibility for a decision that will massively impact your life. You get to make this major decision about *your* life that research tells us will affect what you earn, if and who you marry, and possibly even when and how you will die! So, yes, it's a big decision, but it needn't be a painful process. You do not have to retreat to your room where you'll sweat and cry for several days before emerging looking pale and declaring, 'I'm going to be a librarian.' It's far simpler than that. There's a process that you can follow and like most good processes it has three stages:

1   Background research
2   Trial and error
3   Making a decision and putting it into action.

Doesn't seem so bad, does it? The great thing about this process is that it's actually good fun. You'll learn an awful lot about yourself, meet new people and get to make some mistakes which you will laugh about until your dying day.

At this stage in your career you won't be able to appreciate that this junction in your life is one of blissful possibilities. There will be times in the future when you will want to return to this point (and that's fine, because you can) and enjoy the process of decision making, of researching different careers and of trying them on for fun. So in honour of the future you who is looking jealously at you now, please say with me: 'I don't know what I want to do with my life, but how amazing that I'm going to get the opportunity to find out!'

By doing this you are taking the first step in the background research process: understanding yourself. In all, the research phase contains three steps:

1   Understanding yourself
2   Removing negative influences
3   Creating a longlist.

The rest of this chapter will consider these three steps in turn.

Why you're in this situation (WARNING: contains politics).

Before we get going on our simple three-step process that will lead to your future happiness, let's just take a moment to discover why you're in this position. Why have schools spent a couple of decades honing and refining you as a human being but are prepared to kick you out of the door with no idea of where you want to go next? Well, the answer is part political, part socio-economic and, ultimately, a bit of a mystery.

The political element comes when you consider this little snippet of a speech by Tony Blair way back in the year when we partied like it was 1999 (i.e. 1999):

> "In today's world there is no such thing as too clever. The more you know, the further you will go ... So today I set a target of 50 per cent of young adults going into higher education in the next century."

Guess what? You were one of the young people he was talking about. Blair's comment led to a massive push from government to get 18–30 year olds into higher education. It didn't work. It increased the levels of participation but the closest they ever got was about 39 per cent.

It didn't work largely because of socio-economic reasons. Those being that at the same time as telling young people how terrific higher education was, the government was making it progressively more expensive. It's one thing to have a shiny new government scheme and website outlining how fun and educational going to university can be, but young people are not stupid and when they are also seeing the cost of getting a degree rise to around £53,000 they begin to wonder whether there are alternatives.

As well as getting the big push from government, schools were pushing university. One of the things that schools are judged on is the percentage of people they send to university. The higher this is the better the school is seen to be. Clearly, this doesn't factor in whether a student's future is best served by going to university. Let's consider for a moment a recent survey by City & Guilds, which found that 75 per cent of 14–19 year olds had been informed about university, but only 49 per cent had been told about apprenticeships. It makes you wonder how many of them had been told about sponsored degrees, gap years and getting a job – the chances are that it's less than 49 per cent.

STEP ONE – UNDERSTANDING YOURSELF

The trend for 'finding yourself' seems to have died down a bit since the 1960s (you might want to ask your parents if they travelled or knew any-one who did). 'Finding yourself' (or self-actualisation) was when serious looking hippies would travel to India (they did go to other places but it was almost inevitably India) and try to work out what life was all about through astral meditation and the mind- and bowel-clearing effect of chronic diar-rhoea. Come to think of it there's probably a good reason why the trend hasn't survived. Anyway, the good point about 'finding yourself' was that it was an excellent time for understanding more about what you as a human being were all about. What do you want? What makes you happy? What gets you angry? In effect, your parents' generation allowed themselves a sensible amount of time to understand more about themselves before committing to further levels of education or training. It's worth remembering that if anyone questions your own process of career examination.

REAL LIFE

On the day I turned 30 I had this sudden and overwhelming desire to go to India. I wanted to experience things that were different from what I'd seen so far, something completely and shockingly different. I quit my job, sold everything I owned and bought a ticket. I hated it. I was back at work within a fortnight.

Toby

So how do we find ourselves in this more cynical day and age? Well, we examine ourselves. Not like that, although feel free to do that too. No, we're going to look at what sort of person we are from three different angles:

A   Skills – what am I good at? What can I do well?
B   Motivations – what drives me as a person? What do I want to achieve in life?
C   Passions – what do I love? What makes me happy?

Understanding yourself – skills: what can you do well?

There is often a direct link between what we are good at and what career we are suited to. This could be a skill that we were born with, or it could be something that we've worked at over time. There's no saying that you couldn't develop more skills in the future but for now we want to take a skills audit – this means we're going to list all the skills that we possess. To make it easier we're going to look at two 'levels' of skills: specific skills and general skills.

First we want to look at our **specific skills**. These are usually the things that you get trophies or certificates for. These are abilities that you have which allow you to do something cool. It could be that you can juggle. You might be a black belt in karate, you could know how to fly a plane, you might be a Michelin-starred chef. What you want to put down is the most exhaustive list you possibly can about what skills you have managed to achieve in the time you've been alive. Don't worry about whether things should or shouldn't go on this list – we're aiming for a very long list to start off with and we'll whittle it down later (it's also going to become useful when you start to compile your CV, so it's definitely not time wasted).

ACTION

Turn to the Notes section at the end of the book and add your entries into the My Specific Skills list. If you get stuck, try to think about the following questions:

- O What clubs have you belonged to?
- O What trophies have you got?
- O Have you ever had your name read out in assembly?
- O What do you do outside school?
- O On your social networking profile what do you say about yourself?
- O What do you enjoy?
- O What are your hobbies? What activities do you do at home?

You could also ask your parents and friends what they think you're good at.

The next level is slightly harder to define. **General skills** are the wider skills that we possess. These are more the sorts of things that you will have identified through your years. A good example here is that you might be an incredible juggler, which should be on your specific skills list, but that also shows that you have good co-ordination skills and that you are a performer.

ACTION

Refer to the My General Skills table in the Notes section. Order your general skills in order from one to eight according to how good you are at these particular skills. It's worth knowing that these are taken from a major Confederation of British Industry (i.e. the employers) survey on employability skills. In short they're what employers are looking for from the people they hire. It's well worth making a note of your weaker skills and looking for a way of addressing these shortcomings.

Once you've taken some time to do this you can start to build up a picture of your abilities. Take ten minutes to look at the skills you've acquired – from the list, do any future paths immediately jump out at you? Don't forget that we're not just looking for exact matches here (e.g. you've won several awards for your acting, therefore you should be an actor), we're also looking for general connections. It might be that you never quite realised how many of your skills were connected to your love of communicating. There are loads of careers where this sort of skill could be used and you might like to investigate a few of them.

Understanding yourself – motivations: what makes you get out of bed?

More than any other issue the idea of motivation is perhaps the one that most clearly separates us from other people. Let's take an example. When you write down your skills you may identify that you are a very caring person. If you look at your friends you might notice the same skill in them (as we often tend to become friends with those with a similar outlook to our own). However, there might be a massive gulf between the way that each of you is motivated to employ that skill in your future career. Your friend might want to use their caring nature to nurse sick animals back to health. You might want to use your caring skills to set up your own business that employs counsellors to listen to people's problems. Here then are two caring personalities who are motivated in different ways.

People's motivations are often a cause for some discussion – the more charitable types might think that they're the ones who have the purer motivation, whereas the financially-motivated sorts might characterise the opposite end of the spectrum as hippies. The fact is that no one is 'right'. Our motivations are an enigmatic mixture of all our experiences and our personal ambitions; they are a unique brew and you're arguably better off not knowing why you feel a certain way because it would probably mean lots of expensive therapy. It's also worth noting that our motivations change throughout our life. While you might think that you'd hate working for a massive profits-driven company now, you might feel differently in the future. What is important though is to understand what you feel now and make sure that the future path you choose takes your natural motivations into account.

The other issue when it comes to motivation is to examine your feelings towards money. A good example of how this can change a role is to look at the work of doctors. Some doctors are more motivated by money and they choose to work in the private healthcare industry, where typically salaries are higher. Other doctors may choose to work in the public sector for the NHS and help people who can't afford private healthcare. Again, neither of these choices is 'right' but you have to look at your own feelings on the subject and act accordingly. The other side of the question of money is how you feel about getting a balance between working and living! Do you see work as something that just gets in the way of life, or is it something that you love to do?

REAL LIFE

I made a decision when I was younger that I wanted to retire in my forties, so I chose all of my qualifications based on that. I opted to work longer hours, for companies that I might not otherwise have chosen. It always makes me laugh when I hear someone volunteering talk as if they're the only ones who have value to what they do. I opted to earn more money and I think there's just as much value in that.

Tim

Another interesting thing you may notice from examining your motivation is how you feel about working for others – do you like the idea of being part of a team, of adding your weight to a great company or organisation and helping them achieve something? Or would you rather be the one who is responsible for your own decisions? If it's the latter it could well be that you're more of an entrepreneur who should be the one taking the decisions. Just because you're more entrepreneurial doesn't mean that you're automatically more self-interested. It could be that you want to start up a social enterprise, such as a not-for-profit company, or create your own charity, where all the profits you generate go towards helping other people. Alternatively it could all go into your pocket – it all depends on your personal motivations. Don't judge yourself, just be honest about how you feel.

ACTION

Although you might consider money to be the only measurement that this spectrum is based on, there are other factors. Take a look at the 16 motivational factors that Professor Steven Reiss has highlighted as being the things that shape human behaviour, listed in the Notes section at the end of the book. Ask yourself which of these are motivators for you and which ones don't affect you at all.

Understanding yourself – passions: what do you love?

Do you want to hear the best careers advice that has ever been uttered? It was said by Katherine Whitehorn, who was a journalist and also the Rector of the University of St Andrews. Ready?

> "The best careers advice to give to the young is, 'Find out what you like doing best and get someone to pay you for doing it.'"'

If you can understand the truth of that quotation then the rest of this book could be absolutely blank and you would still be equipped with the knowledge you need to go ahead and secure the best future for yourself. The reason that Whitehorn was so incredibly right is that her advice touches on something that we don't often like to talk about – we are all going to die. Now, it's fair enough that you didn't come to this book to be confronted with that sort of talk, so apologies, but it's a truth – perhaps the only truth (although others maintain that death and taxes are the only inevitable things).

Despite how it sounds, the knowledge that you're going to pop your clogs is really rather brilliant. It means that this life you are leading and these mere moments you are alive for are incredibly important. They represent the only chance you'll ever, ever have of being here and doing something, doing anything. So it stands to reason that how you spend that time is important. Therefore it would be a criminal waste if you were to spend even a fraction of your one and only and precious life doing something you didn't want to do. So don't – instead follow Whitehorn's advice and find out what you like doing best. Resolve here and now to honour your imminent death by spending your life doing things that you love. Melodramatic? Certainly. But it's true – committing to pursuing your own path despite fear or peer pressure is the recipe for a happy life.

One issue that might be holding you back is that too many people focus on the other side of Whitehorn's advice and become convinced that they could never find someone to pay them to play *Call of Duty* for the rest of their life. However, this is overlooking the fact that if you absolutely love playing games, then you might like to look at the range of careers that are available in Britain's booming games industry. OK, so you might not get to play games all day long but you would be surrounded by them, you would be creating them, you would be immersed in the world that you love, and that sounds pretty impressive, right? You might love eating, skiing, collecting ceramic cats – all of these passions can suggest several career paths from the literal (chef, competitive skier, grandmother) to the connected (food writer, travel agent, auctioneer).

ACTION

Forget rational thought – turn to the Notes section and write down what you love doing. At least ten things that make you incredibly happy. Take some time to create this list and then review it – what does it point towards? Don't worry about finding the literal connection. Stuck? Answer these questions:

- What makes you happy?
- If you won the lottery tomorrow, what would you do for the rest of your days?
- What do you think is important?
- Forget obligations and what you have to do – what do you want to do?
- Whose job interests you?
- Who inspires you?

All of this research is fantastic for getting the details you need to build up a picture of you as a person and work out what will fit with you. However, there's a very important step that you need to take next.

STEP TWO – REMOVING NEGATIVE INPUT AND ADDING POSITIVE INFLUENCES

You've had lessons about peer pressure since you were young. When your parents were chastising you for being dragged along by a crowd they would intone that classic parental rant, 'Would you jump off a cliff just because X did?' There's no doubting that outside influences play a massive part in our career decisions and often they're not entirely positive. It's healthy to get other perspectives on an issue, but the final answer has to come from your own point of view or else you're not pursuing your own path.

What follows are some of the sources of influence that you're probably under the sway of to a greater or lesser extent. Knowing what influences there are on your career can help you to tune them out so that it's only your own voice that is responsible for making the important decisions that are coming up.

Your family

Did you know that, according to a survey by the Warwick Junior Commission, 53 per cent of children claimed to want a job like their parents and 60 per cent of A-level choices were in either similar or the same subjects as those their parents took? Coincidence? Hardly. You can make the case that it's possibly because you share the same skills and motivations as your parents do that so many of us end up in the same career, but there are other reasons too. It could be that your parents' careers are one of the few that you've ever actually been exposed to. It's always easier to take the route that you know rather than a new and possibly frightening one. Weirdly some people still think this even if the destination isn't one they want to go to.

Funnily enough, even the name that your parents choose for you can influence what you go on to do. It's called nominative determinism and it's been studied (seriously!) to see how much influence it has on our career choices – statistically it does have an effect. So if your surname is Baker then you might like to think about whether your decision to get into making bread was really yours or was preordained. Sort of makes you wonder why you never meet anyone called Mr Careersadvisor.

Another way your parents influence your career choices is through what they say. Whether they undermine you or encourage you, they have probably been voicing opinions about your career for several years. It's precisely these opinions that we have to try to delete. It can be useful to get other people's opinions but ultimately it's your views that count. If there are expectations that you go on to do a certain thing, whether it's a family career that everyone follows or simply something that other people have decided for you, it's time to break out of the mould. Watch *Billy Elliott* and get inspired that regardless of our parents' expectations of us, we should all feel the responsibility to do what we love – you're dying remember!

Friends

There's safety in numbers and it's a documented fact that school leavers sometimes just follow the crowd. It could be that you follow the crowd to university, or into work, but again you have to break the cycle of influence so that your decision is **YOUR** decision. We also match ourselves up to an unwritten and unspoken expectation of what we go on to do after school. For many it's seen as the inevitable progression that you will leave school and go on to university. When we do these things unthinkingly we often end up making mistakes. It's often not a huge amount of fun to examine ourselves and inspect our true reasons for doing something, as it involves work and possibly having to make a different choice, but unless you want to waste time, money and your life then you have to break out of this complacency.

REAL LIFE

I didn't just choose my university based on where my friends were going, but also my course! It's embarrassing to admit it now but I just felt it would be easier and safer to go and study with people I knew than do something on my own. With hindsight I can see that it was a massive waste of time – why didn't I just choose something I really wanted to do? What was I so scared of?

Kym

Other influences

Take a look at the following list and see if you can spot the ones that have influenced your own decision:

○ Grandparents – have they always wanted their little grandson or granddaughter to be something in particular?
○ Geography – does everyone in your area specialise in a particular trade? Do you have to be the same?
○ Teachers – did a teacher you know and trust say that they thought you should go to university? Is that right for you?

○ TV/films/media – sounds crazy doesn't it but there's always been a connection between which TV programmes are popular and the take-up of courses. So every new series of *CSI* means the forensic science courses are oversubscribed.

Once you've established which particular voices are the loudest when it comes to your career choices, you'll get a better idea of the pressures you're under to make a particular decision. No one likes letting people down and it may be that you can't escape some influences, but you have to at least understand that this decision is yours and yours alone. If people react badly when you announce what it is that you're interested in doing next, then take it as a sign that they have their own agenda for what you should do.

They might think you're wrong but you have to let them know that you are thinking for yourself. It's always worth having a well-thought-out structure to your arguments. This is especially true with parents, who may feel they have the most right to tell you that you're making the wrong decision. But ultimately they have to accept that you are old enough to make your own decisions and to live with the consequences.

ACTION

Turn to the Notes section and write down three sources of influence that you've experienced on your own career choices. Try to identify what it is that *they* want you to do. It's vital that you can see how these voices are influencing your own.

Collecting good influences

There is an exception to our rule – a group of people who you should absolutely allow yourself to be influenced by, because they are trained to do exactly that. This army of highly trained experts are called careers advisors and they are absolutely on your side. But they are human. They have different opinions and they sometimes get things wrong, which is why you should look to get the input of at least two or better still three careers advisors. You can access them for free through www.nextstep. direct.gov.uk. You can access them over the web, over the phone and in person. You should try all of these things. The more information you can get at this stage the better.

They might even do some occupational testing, which will be based on your skills and motivations (so you'll have a headstart). Don't feel though that just because a computer program spits out a particular career that you are in any way obliged to take this route. Again though, these websites and programs can give you useful information to compile your longlist.

STEP THREE – CREATING A LONGLIST

A longlist is a list that is longer than a shortlist. Well, duh! Your career path longlist is going to be at least 20 careers long. It's compiled from a range of sources and is designed to ensure that it will help you to investigate a range of future options. If you want to have more than 20 choices that's fine, but aim for fewer than 50 careers or you'll never have time to investigate them all properly.

ACTION

Turn to the Notes section and, using your lists of skills/ motivations/passions and the input of different sources, make a list of at least 20 career paths you want to investigate in more detail. Where are these career paths coming from?

○ Ask your parents to suggest three things they think you would be good at.

○ Ask your friends to suggest three careers they think you would be good at.

○ Take as many careers as you can from your general and specific skills.

○ Add in the careers from TV, books, films, the media and the world around you.

○ Add in the careers that the various careers advisors suggested.

○ Remember to add in at least five random choices. It doesn't matter how you come up with them. Flick through job profiles on Next Step and pick a couple. Flick through the *Yellow Pages* and stop randomly and pick a couple. Think of friends' parents and add a couple of their careers.

Now look at your list. Isn't that cool? You've got a huge longlist of things that you can potentially end up doing. Finally, don't forget to say out loud:

> "I don't know what I want to do with my life, but how amazing that I'm going to get the opportunity to find out!"

HOW FAR DO YOU WANT TO GO IN BUSINESS?

THE CHARTERED ACCOUNTANT. NO ONE'S BETTER QUALIFIED.

London, Shanghai, New York, Singapore?
ICAEW Chartered Accountants have the work experience,
financial intelligence and skills the business world demands.

**Become 'chartered' and start your journey
at icaew.com/betterqualified**

ICAEW

A WORLD LEADER OF THE ACCOUNTANCY AND FINANCE PROFESSION

CHAPTER TWO

FROM LONGLIST TO SHORTLIST TO A DECISION

This chapter in brief

- Going from longlist to shortlist to a decision is as simple as rejecting everything that isn't perfectly right for you.

- Online research is a great way to sort the job facts from the job fiction.

- Offline research means taking your shortlist of jobs into the real world.

- Making mistakes is an essential part of the process.

If you followed the advice in Chapter 1 and everything went to plan (if it didn't, see the Tip box below), you will now have a longlist of potential futures that you want to investigate. This chapter will teach you how to 'try on' all of those different futures from your longlist. In much the same way that you'd never spend £200 on a pair of trousers without seeing if they fit, why would you spend tens of thousands of pounds on training yourself for a career that you're not even sure you would enjoy? That's a rhetorical question by the way – you wouldn't do that, it would be madness (as is spending £200 on trousers).

But before we take our metaphorical trousers into the changing room, there's some work that needs to be done. How did we reach this point? Sticking with the metaphor of trousers – how have you ended up in this particular shop looking at these particular trousers in the first place? If you're a smart shopper, perhaps you looked online first to see what sort of trousers a particular shop was selling. Maybe you saw someone wearing some amazing trousers in the street and asked them where they got them from. However you did it, you need to narrow down the field before you go and try on – there's just too many trousers out there to try them all on.

Perhaps that's enough of trousers. Fortunately, it's exactly the same with your longlist of careers – before you head out into the real world to try some of them on you're going to spend some time on a nice comfy sofa with a cup of tea, several biscuits and a good broadband connection. So fetch your longlist of futures, your laptop and bear in mind that when he was sculpting *David*, Michelangelo was asked how he could have created a statue so perfect, his reply is great advice for the careers researcher: 'I just cut away everything that wasn't David.' This is exactly what you're going to do next – cut away the bits that aren't absolutely perfect for you. We do this using two levels of filtering:

O Online research
O Real world research.

'Help! I still don't have a longlist of jobs'

If you still don't have a longlist of 20 futures you want to investigate, this is for you. In Chapter 1 we looked at two stages to help us understand ourselves.

This involved learning more about what sort of a person you are:

1   Skills – what are you good at?
2   Motivations – what gets you out of bed in the morning? Do you want riches or to help the world?
3   Passions – what do you love to do?

We then looked at removing the filters that sometimes influence us away from the things that we really want – this could be our parents, our teachers, our friends or where we live. It's OK to have those influences around us as long as we understand that they are not our own choices.

After these two stages, we went searching for some good advice. We took our knowledge about ourselves, our skills, motivations and passions and spoke to a number of good careers advisors. We also added in a few possible futures from some more random sources and generated our longlists.

There's no real shortcut past this process. You can cheat – of course you can – you can ask your friends what they got, or you can just pick all 20 at random, but without doing a bit of research first it's unlikely that you'll get the right ones. So you'll potentially miss out on the right future for you. Still can't be bothered? We have prepared a lazy person's longlist (see below) based on some of the most popular career choices advisors get

PROPERTY OF MERTHYR
TYDFIL PUBLIC LIBRARIES

asked about, so you'll notice that it's really general. Feel free to start with this list and then get more specific. Better still, head back to Chapter 1 and create a list that's perfect for you.

The lazy longlist

1	Sales	10	Farmer
2	Computing	11	Marketing/advertising
3	Human resources	12	Artist
4	Starting your own business	13	Police/fire service
5	Joining the armed forces	14	Nursery
		15	Social work
6	Tourism	16	Product designer
7	Mechanic	17	Lawyer
8	Doctor	18	Accountant
9	Customer services	19	Teacher
		20	Plumber

ONLINE RESEARCH

Are you sitting comfortably? Then let's begin. The aim of this online research is to gather a series of facts about a career that will allow you to judge whether it's right for you. As a member of a generation that has never known a time pre-Google (it was awful), you're probably already aware that there's a good deal of information out there on the internet. However, you're possibly also aware that there's a lot of really terrible information masquerading as good information out there too. A good way to get around this problem is to look for more than one source of information (three actually) and then compare. Once you do that it's usually easy to spot which one is out of sync with the others.

ACTION ⚡

Start a new folder on your computer called something obvious like 'Career Research'. Inside this folder you should start a new folder for each of your 20 longlisted careers. Inside each of these folders you can start a Word document named after the particular future you're investigating. In this document you're going to be pasting a lot of information. It's important that you've got all of this information in one place because it's the simplest way of being able to compare things side by side.

If at any point you're thinking that this is a bit too much like hard work, then remember that this research is not only going to help you choose a particular career but will also help you get into your chosen future and give you a better chance of succeeding. Think of it like coursework that will actually help you to get a job and live a happier life.

So what information do we want to find and paste into this document? And where can we start searching for it?

1   Job profiles
2   Case studies
3   Contacts.

Job profiles

A job profile is the simple background information that explains what a particular job entails, how much you can potentially earn, how you get into that particular job and lots of other information around it, such as working hours and whether there is a recognised industry body that is responsible for this particular profession.

These are the basic pieces of information that you need to establish in order to understand more about the job or future. It's quite common to find that something that you assumed was true about a job is far from the reality. For example, the glamour that people assume comes with working in PR or TV might disguise the fact that you'd be expected to work for very little money in the beginning and put in long hours. You might not even get invited to the parties until a lot later in your career. Searching out the information to create your own job profiles will help you establish careers fact from careers fiction.

Here are three good places to start finding some information – the fourth you probably already knew about:

1   http://www.prospects.ac.uk/types_of_jobs.htm
2   https://nextstep.direct.gov.uk/planningyourcareer/jobprofiles/Pages/
     default.aspx
3   http://www.totaljobs.com/careers-advice/inside-careers/job-profiles/
     account-manager
4   Google UK – 'your chosen career' + job profile.

Although it will require a lot of cutting and pasting, you'll start to build up a detailed picture of each of the roles. Read through the information carefully and see if you can get an idea of whether or not this role *feels* like you.

REAL LIFE

I wanted to work in film from when I was young because I imagined that the actors must be incredibly exciting and interesting people. I now work in film and love it, but by far the most exciting and interesting people are the crew! Actors are incredibly vain, which makes sense because they spend all day being looked at.

Gill

Case studies

Besides the job profile, case studies are the most useful things that you can locate when it comes to your career research. Just as a job profile will help you establish the facts regarding a particular career, case studies should help you work out how closely the truth follows the written word of the profile. In most cases you'll find that although there are so-called facts about a job these are not set in stone – for example, there may be an accepted way to get into the industry but plenty of people make their way in through a separate route. This is the gold that you're panning for. You want to find the insights that other people doing this research won't get if they accept the authorised versions of things. Again the key is to look for a few different sources:

1   http://www.notgoingtouni.co.uk/beinspired/index
2   http://www.prospects.ac.uk/case_studies.htm
3   YouTube – search 'your chosen career' + case study.

ACTION

Before we undertake the final stage of the pruning process, which is a bit more time consuming, it's time for a cull of your longlist. At this stage we're looking to halve the longlist down to ten careers. What most people find is that there are a few that instantly stand out as candidates for rejection. If that's the case, bin those (although keep the careers research in case you want to revisit it at a place later on in your career). Then it's a matter of putting them in order and selecting the ten that most closely fit your requirements for a perfect job. Try not to worry too much about selecting the wrong ones – if you feel strongly about one aspect of a job put it on your new longlist and say goodbye to the ones you're less keen on.

TIP ✓

Presenting a personal image that people will hire/not fire

This is the stage in the process where you are about to go beyond the online research and get out and interact in the real world. To get the absolute maximum out of all encounters, both online and offline, there are a few simple rules to ensure you present a pleasant, professional image.

- **Go smart, then dress down**. A suit, shirt and tie is never the wrong thing to wear. It is much easier to make a suit and tie look far less formal than it is to make jeans and a T-shirt look smart.

- **This applies to language too**. Start off as formally as you possibly can (that means switching on the spellcheck, paying attention to grammar and banishing the smilies) and get more comfortable when the other person does. Never be the first to LOL.

- **People are always watching**. Whether it's your Facebook profile, your Twitter feed or the things you're saying in the canteen, people are always watching. Your behaviour is no longer being judged by your mates and teachers, it's being scrutinised by employers who have the power to hire or fire you. Always assume that someone is watching you and act accordingly. Either keep your online profiles extremely private or accept that whatever you put there can be seen or found. Choose a businesslike email – thedirtycrunkster@hotmail.co.uk won't get you too many interviews.

- **Be polite and helpful**. You can have all the degrees and PhDs in the world but if you're rude, don't help others or don't say please and thank you then you'll always struggle to get on, and rightly so.

Collecting contacts

The final stage of your sofa research is to establish a rough group of contacts for these different areas. The point of this is to find at least two people for your remaining careers who you can email or call. You should be able to approach them to get more information and start to build up your network of contacts within the industry. You are looking for people who have worked in the industry or role you're looking at for a good length of time. New starters are fine too but they won't have the extensive networks that people who have been in the job for longer will have. When you have a choice of who to ask for, pick the CEO or managing director. These are the people at the top and will have the most influence within the business, enabling them to answer your question or invite you into the business.

How do you find these contacts?

It can be helpful to have a new bookmark folder for each future you are researching and start bookmarking the various different sites you find that are of interest. It's also very useful to start using and maintaining a proper contacts system. Most email programs have an address book function and you can add people to that and usually add notes. Record the person's name, occupation and notes about the relationship such as what you've asked them for and when. This might sound like a long-winded process but over the course of a career it will repay you many times over.

The first step is to ask the people you know (relatives, friends, organisations you belong to such as sporting clubs, churches, etc.) if they know of anyone in the ten areas in which you're looking to find contacts. Explain politely why you're looking for these contacts and ask them if they would be OK about you getting in touch with them to ask some questions at some point. If they agree and are happy for you to contact the person directly, ask for a contact email and telephone.

The contacts that come from someone who knows you are the strongest introductions you can get. This is because when you get in touch you can say something like, 'I hope you don't mind me emailing/calling you but _____ said that you might be OK answering some questions for some research I'm doing for my career.' The use of that person's name is your foot in the door. It also makes it especially important that you remain polite, otherwise you're damaging not only your reputation but also the reputation of the person who introduced you.

As well as speaking to people face to face, you could try emailing or making the most of social networking. Finally, all those hours on Facebook are about to pay off! Twitter is fantastic for finding people by their occupation as directories such as wefollow.com and Twellow.com list people by their job title. If they tweet about their job you can read back through their timeline and get a first-hand account of the frustrations and joys of working in a particular business. LinkedIn is another superb tool for careers research. You can find groups that contain nothing but people who work in a particular industry; many of those industry groups have sub-groups for people looking to get work in an area. Facebook can be useful too – not only can you find individuals but groups and companies will usually have a page too. Just by connecting to them you can start to research people who could be of use (just remember to see the earlier points on presenting a professional image).

While you're finding contacts online you could try checking out the website for an industry body. Wikipedia has useful lists of both 'trade associations' and 'professional associations in the United Kingdom'. Once you've found the relevant organisation you should read through their website. It's likely that they will have an FAQ for people who are looking to get information on the industry – they might even provide a contact. Many will also have forums that you can join up to – but remember the above point about online conduct, even in a supposedly anonymous forum.

What do you do with these contacts?

Once you've got a couple of contacts for each of the ten roles you're researching, it's time to consider what you want to find out from these contacts. As ever, be polite in your approach and conduct, but you can use these contacts as the sounding board for your questions. Read back through the research you've accumulated and work out what it is that you really want to know. Try to limit your questions to no more than five when approaching your contacts – if you send over too many basic questions then you might make them feel that you're asking them to do your careers research for you. *Never* send out a standard email containing vague questions to all your contacts, they'll know what you're doing and they'll hate it.

ACTION

Approach your contacts for the different industries to get the final information you need on a particular career. Be polite and appreciate the time that you are asking these people to give you. If you've been introduced by someone, always mention them (and say thank you for the introduction). Here are some possible questions you could ask your contacts:

- What is their advice for getting into the industry, based on your circumstances?
- What progression is possible within a job?
- How should you sell yourself to particular employers?
- What qualifications are actually useful in the job?
- Do employers prefer some universities to others?
- Are there alternative routes in?
- Do they know of any boom areas in this particular role?
- What will be the growth areas with this job in the coming years?

After this much research you will probably have had a good number of shocks as you've read, seen and heard from reliable sources that some of the things you thought were true about a particular job aren't as clear cut. You may have realised as you've looked through all the information that you couldn't work for that sort of salary, or that you're intrigued by a particular route. Take your time. Re-read your research. Be honest with your feelings and thoughts and let the information soak in. If at any point you feel you need more details on a particular career head back to your contacts and talk until you get it.

Using this information it should be possible to look at the remaining ten careers on your longlist and strike five of them off to create a five job shortlist. As you did before, reject the ones that seem like they're not such a good fit for your personality (re-read your skills, motivations and passions list if you need to) and highlight the ones that make you genuinely excited. When you truly feel that glimmer of excitement about a career then you'll know you've done your research well.

ACTION

Update the Notes section with the five careers that contain some element that genuinely makes you excited. Don't fake it – if all of them leave you cold and you're really not feeling even a glimmer of excitement about any of them then don't panic. It could well be that you either need more time to go through the research, or you've still not hit upon the right career for you. If that's the case look through the elements of the job research that you've done and identify three aspects that made you hopeful and excited. Take these back to a careers advisor and ask them to suggest roles based on those elements. Then go back through the online research phase with this new list. You're absolutely not wasting your time – every time you highlight another element you like or reject another job option, you're getting closer to that five careers shortlist that really makes you excited.

GOING FROM FIVE TO ONE WITH REAL WORLD RESEARCH

You have in your hand a list of five possible futures and, understandably, you want to narrow that down and find out which one is right for you. It's likely that whichever path you choose will require a sizeable amount of investment afterwards in the form of further training, and possibly other forms of investment too. Fortunately, as a Not Going To Uni reader you will be far better prepared than the average person, because not only have you done your online research but you're also about to go out into the real world and try the careers on for yourself. How do you do that then?

There are four main ways of getting hands-on experience of a job or a particular future:

1   Work shadowing
2   Work experience placement
3   Volunteering
4   Getting a job.

ICAEW

A world leader of the accountancy and finance profession

Rachael

One of the things that put me off going to university was the debt I would have accrued. I liked the idea of earning while I learn! I initially considered a career in textiles however I realised my focus had shifted and that it wasn't the creative side of textiles I was interested in, but the business side.

Despite being offered a place at the University of Southampton to study management, I decided to take a gap year to look at other options, which is when I discovered that some of the bigger firms were beginning to offer school-leaver programmes. In particular Deloitte's BrightStart programme caught my eye and following my application, various tests, interviews and an assessment day, I was selected to become part of the first ever BrightStart intake in September 2011.

I am currently working as part of a team on different audit projects on a week-by-week basis. In between times I then study at college for the internationally-recognised ACA qualification. I'm constantly working with different clients in all kinds of sectors so it's never boring! I would recommend a programme like this to anyone who is looking for an alternative route into chartered accountancy, who doesn't necessarily want to go to university.

Thomas

The percentage of FTSE 100 boards that have ACA qualified chartered accountants was a huge attraction for me when looking into potential professional qualifications.

In addition to this, the AAT-ACA Fast Track scheme was also a reason for me choosing the ACA qualification as instead of incurring student debt, I was able to earn and save my money. This enabled me to take some fantastic holidays!

I am now an Audit Principal and work for the National Audit Office, playing an important part in helping to ensure that the Government is held accountable to Parliament for the way it uses public money. A typical day doesn't exist and I can be anywhere from the office in London, to visiting clients in other parts of the country or indeed Europe.

The most difficult aspect of training to be an ICAEW Chartered Accountant via the AAT-ACA Fast Track has been balancing work commitments and study. However I don't have any regrets about not going to university and I feel perhaps even at a slight advantage to my peers who did go to university, as I have had four years of additional experience working for the National Audit Office.

For more information visit
www.icaew.com

What's the difference and what do you choose for which role?

A work shadow is essentially career stalking and it's brilliant not only for getting your foot in the door with a company, but also for letting you ask questions and experience the work of someone doing the thing that you want to do. A work shadow can be as little as half a day and involves you piggy-backing (not literally) on someone's day and helping out where possible. It's first-hand exposure to the realities of a job, albeit over a short space of time. Again it's priceless for giving you the industry contacts and to show that you're a good bet for future employment.

A work experience placement is a formalised (as in there's often contracts involved) process that brings you into a company for a set period of time, often a week, a month, a summer or an entire year (often known as a year in industry, or a placement year). Longer placements may involve some form of payment.

By contrast volunteering is where you give yourself up as free labour to a particular cause or concern. Most volunteering takes place within charities or public sector organisations and involves you undertaking unpaid work, usually because it's something you believe in, or it's a good way of building up your experience of a particular industry or profession.

Getting a job might seem like a rather extreme form of testing out a career but think about it. Let's say you think your future is in sales but you're not quite sure. Now, you could go to university, spend £50,000, do a business degree, wait three years and then start applying, get a job in sales and start work only to find that you absolutely hate it. Or you could get a temp job or a Saturday job that involves some element of selling (temp work in a mobile phone shop, for example). This could give you enough information to let you know that actually you find it hideously embarrassing and it's not the job for you.

If you are offered work experience then by all means take it, but don't be afraid to ask for exposure to more than one role. The best forms of work experience should involve both the recruiter and the student being very clear about what they want from the placement. The employer might want something relatively menial like data entry done, and the student might want exposure to the work of the marketing department. You should say what you're looking for and be explicit about what you want. After all, there's not much point simply signing up and hoping that you get what you want. You might, but the smart move would be to arrange it in advance so that the process works for you.

REAL LIFE

The best work experience I ever had was working in a sandwich delivery company one summer. It sounds crazy but we got to go into every different type of business and I saw and learned about industries I didn't even know existed. You could also see which industries attracted the real idiots. On top of that I also got free sandwiches!

Bao

The options above have been arranged in terms of the time and effort that it typically takes to organise each experience. For that reason it makes sense to see if you can start off with work shadowing in each particular role and then progress depending on how you find each experience. You might be thinking that it would take a lot to sort out five separate work shadows but as each shadow might only last a day you're really only looking at an investment of around ten days, if you do two shadows for each career.

How do you arrange work shadowing?

Go back to your careers research and target in a bit more on the contacts that you started to develop. Provided you left the relationship on a good footing, it's a good idea to start with them. What you need is a sensible proposition that you can email or post (some companies will need things like this in writing) to them. The key here is to go to the top, aim for the CEOs and the managers who aren't going to have to get permission to let someone into the building for a day, and approach them in a professional and mature way. The following template email gives you an idea of how to explain clearly what you are doing and what you want from this person.

Hello,

As you know I'm currently in the process of researching my career options and one of the things that I'm really interested in is the work of CAREER TYPE X. I've been looking into this because I've always been a very X sort of person and even won X [some sort of evidence that shows how you have been made for this role].

I'd really like to see what the job actually involves. Would it be possible to arrange a work shadow where I could come in for a day, or even half a day and just observe what it is that the job involves? I'd welcome any thoughts or advice you have.

I fully appreciate you're very busy but it would make a massive difference to helping me decide what to do for the rest of my life and potentially what to go on and study when I leave school. I'm very flexible with regard to times and would really appreciate your help.

Yours sincerely,

YOUR NAME

This will be successful more times than you might think. You'll either get some interesting feedback in the form of an email, or you'll get the all-important shadow. Because this is so effective you should really start with the companies that genuinely take your interest. If you had the complete freedom to choose, which company would you work for? Ask yourself why that is. Then explain that you've thought about this in your introductory email. This is where you should let them see the genuine excitement you have for the job – they might well find it refreshing to meet someone who is not cynical! Never feel that you're not worth these people's time. Regardless of their wealth, fame or position in society, you are a human being who is politely asking for a reasonable favour. If they're too busy then they'll say so – you politely accept it and move on (perhaps end the conversation by asking who they think you could approach), but not to ask in the first place is unforgivable!

When you get your work shadow it's vital that you a) turn up and look pre-sentable and b) have thought about some questions you'd like to know the answers to. Bring a notepad and a pen and take notes of things that interest you. Don't interrupt; be conscious that this person has invited you into their working world and you are a guest, so be on your best behaviour. You should also understand that you should treat any busi-ness information you are privy to as completely private.

Remember names of people and take their business cards if they offer you one. Following the shadow it's both polite and sensible to return to these people and build on the introduction. Even if it's just a brief email that says it was good to meet them and thank them for the time. You could even ask if they would mind in future if you got in contact if there was something that came up. Ninety-nine percent of people will not have a problem with it, and at that point you've recruited another person to your network, so make another entry into the address book and marvel at your expanding career network.

Plan your experience strategy

However you look at it you'll want to make sure you get some form of exposure to your five potential futures. In an ideal world you should try to get at least two for each future because it could be that you have one exposure to one future and hate it because of the hours, the environment or even just a difficult commute. In the same way that we wouldn't trust one source of information from the internet, we shouldn't make a decision about something in life based on one experience.

Planning your strategy should be a very conscious thing. You should sit down and work out how you'll get your exposures to these roles and when. It's worth committing to exploring all five possibilities even if you absolutely love the first one, as you quite possibly will. Equally, if the first exposure is a bit depressing then don't give up on the process – you're so close to the final hurdle and progressing to the next stage, which is selecting your training.

TIP ✔

Mentors

The idea of mentors seems to be something that has lost favour in recent years, but the mentoring/mentee relationship is one that has worked for millennia and there's no reason why you can't benefit from it too. The notion of mentors is probably now most widely known in kung fu movies, where a young and naïve trainee is mentored by a wizened old black belt who passes on all the secret knowledge that he's acquired through the years. That, in essence, is the mentoring process, although it's unlikely that your mentor will teach you the Vibrating Palm of Death.

So how can you use mentors? Well, you can ask people to mentor you, which means that they accept some responsibility for your development. In many ways it simply formalises a relationship between you and an important contact. If you come into contact with someone in your network who you really feel understands your situation and what you want to do, but also has the skills and experience that you want, then you could ask them to mentor you. It's a huge compliment that you can pay someone who is progressing in their career and the chances are that they will be flattered, but also a bit concerned about what it will entail. The answer is that it can involve absolutely anything you want but it has to be agreed between you.

A typical mentoring arrangement might be that you would have an initial meeting to discuss the terms of the mentorship and what you both hope to get out of it (never forget that this should be a two-way process, the mentor should say what they want too). You could then arrange a regular meeting (even if it was once every term, or even once a year) and establish a channel for communications – most likely to agree that an email correspondence would be of use.

Typically, you could then explain to your mentor what your career position is and outline any challenges that you feel are coming up. Your mentor would then give their perspective on these challenges and potentially suggest some routes forward. You shouldn't think that your mentor exists to solve your problems, they are simply a very well-placed resource who you can run things past.

It may well be that your mentor helps you to achieve your aims, by opening their network to you or putting in a word for you, but all of this depends on you developing the relationship – prove your value and your mentor could end up giving you something even cooler than the Vibrating Palm of Death.

'I KNOW WHAT I WANT TO DO'

Wow. In just two chapters you've gone from a tantrum to a fully researched professional-in-waiting with experience under your belt, the beginnings of a network in your chosen area and a much clearer idea of what is right for you, who you are and what you want to achieve. You might even have found a mentor or a contact who can help you get where you want to go. Wow!

Don't forget that even if you have an absolute concrete belief that this is the right choice for you now, the key element of that sentence is 'now' – in three years, five years, a decade, twenty years you might not feel the same. Fortunately, given what you've learned in the last two chapters, you also know what to do if you find yourself dissatisfied – you simply start to understand yourself, remove the filters, do your research, try things on and then make your move. Never again will you have to get frustrated and shout: 'I don't know what I want to do!'

ACTION

This is it. Take a final look at your notes and research and think about the experiences you've had while organising your work placements. It's time to whittle down those five potential futures and select just one. This is really simple: pick the one that makes you the most excited – over the course of your working life that excitement will be priceless. Congratulations, you've now found what it is that you love – the next step is finding someone to pay you to do it.

From your career research you should have identified the most common routes into the industry, and your contacts and case studies might have given you a reality check, so you know there's more to do, or alternative routes in. It's highly likely that your next steps will require more training and over the next few chapters we will look at some of the most common forms of training. We will give you the inside secrets on how to make the most of them, how to get them cheaper or for free, and how to create your own routes into any career you want.

'I STILL DON'T KNOW WHAT I WANT TO DO!'

Have you read the last few chapters and done the work? If you have and you're still unsure it's quite possible that you just need more time to repeat the process over a wider range of possible futures. Fortunately, there's no real rush. Read Chapter 3 and consider taking a gap year. This will buy you some more of the world's most precious commodity: time.

Not going to uni?

love FOOD?

Then why not consider a career in the food and drink industry - it's got lots to offer!

You could be developing a new range of breakfast cereals, taste testing ice creams or creating an advertising campaign for soft drinks - there's no shortage of options and exciting opportunities!

Pay and prospects are good and many employers pay you well whilst helping you to gain the qualifications you need.

Careers in the food industry are exciting, challenging and there's never a dull moment

A FUTURE IN FOOD

TASTE SUCCESS

About Us

The 'Taste Success – A Future in Food' campaign is run by UK food and drink manufacturers to tell you about the wide range of great career opportunities available.

Find out more at: www.tastesuccess.co.uk

CHAPTER THREE

THE GAP YEAR IS DEAD, LONG LIVE THE R&D YEAR

This chapter in brief

- The term gap year is out of date and unhelpful. Instead of a gap year, think about taking a research and development (R&D) year.

- Everyone, regardless of education, class or gender, should at least consider taking an R&D year.

- R&D years aren't just about travelling, they're about researching your future career and developing your skills, employability and personal profile.

- That might well mean travelling.

- The key to convincing others to let you take an R&D year lies in emphasising the practical benefits it could give you.

For such a positive experience, gap years have managed to attract a lot of negative baggage (see the Tip box below). Part of the problem is the name. Think about it – where else is the notion of a gap a good thing? Certainly not in dentistry and any traveller worth their salt knows that you have to MIND THE GAP. If you're trying to sell the notion of taking a gap year to your parents it's quite likely that they'll hear the word 'gap' and think of falling behind and a desperate race to catch up.

That's why the gap year has to die. Instead we think that you should consider a research and development (R&D) year. What's the difference? Well, a gap year is when the Ruperts and Jocastas of this world go off on a £30k holiday where they build schools for elephants. A research and development year is a period of time when you can make a considered judgement about what to do next, but it's also a phase when you can develop yourself – as a person, a potential employee and a human being. Who could possibly object to that?

In fact the gap year has attracted so many myths and untruths that you might be thinking of skipping this chapter, because you've already decided that it's not for you. That's fine. Feel free to skip ahead – provided you read and understand the information here:

TIP ✔

Five myths about gap years

1   *They're just for rich kids* – no, they're not.
2   *They cost a lot of money* – no, they don't, otherwise they'd just be for rich kids and we've just said that they're not.
3   *They mean travelling* – no, they don't. Thousands of school leavers take a gap year and stay within a 40-mile radius of their own bed.

4   *Your parents would not let you take one* – what? You really think your parents would object to you improving your employability, learning new skills and building up your life experiences?

5   *They are a waste of time* – absolutely NOT. In fact, a gap year could actually save your life.

Still want to skip the chapter?

SO WHAT IS AN R&D YEAR THEN, AND HOW COULD IT SAVE YOUR LIFE?

In a perfect world, all of the work and research that we've outlined in the first two chapters – the exercises and questions that refine your ideas about potential futures and guide you towards making informed choices – would be done while you were still at school. That would mean that you could get to your school graduation ceremony and annoy everyone by saying with confidence that you know precisely what you want to do next and that you're genuinely excited about the future. However, you've probably noticed that school is busy. Alongside lessons and exams quite a lot of other stuff happens. Friends, girlfriends, boyfriends (or both), parties, music, books, cinema, work and revision all tend to get in the way. As John Lennon once remarked, 'Life is what happens to you while you're busy making other plans.'

So what happens if you get to the end of school and you still haven't had the time to make the right decision? You take an R&D year. And one of the things that you do during that year is your career research and figure out what's really right for you. That way, rather than going off and getting a qualification in something you don't want to do and building up debt that it takes decades to get rid of, you will make a better choice and, ultimately, avoid wasting your life. Add in the fact that you'll have some amazing life experiences (which can be sold to parents and future employers as ultimate skill-enhancing opportunities) and you've got an unbeatable combination.

REAL LIFE

I had no idea what to do when I left school so rather than taking the time to figure out what was right for me I just did the first course I could find at the uni where my girlfriend went. We split up in the first year and I hated the course. It took me three years to get back to where I was when I left school!

Pete

DEFERRING — A SMART MOVE

Deferring means asking for your university place to be held over until the next academic year. So rather than starting in September 2012, you'd start in September 2013, for instance. It doesn't cost anything to defer, although you need to be aware that you might end up paying the fees at the 2013 rates, rather than 2012 – so keep an eye out for more increases. Based on the latest figures around 7 per cent, approximately 33,000 students, defer their place at university. Over the last decade this has risen from around 28,000, so we can safely say that R&D years are an increasingly popular option.

In fact, most universities are in favour of deferment because they know that it can save you making the wrong choices, as the University of Roehampton states on its website: 'We welcome students who wish to defer entry, and believe that applicants who decide to broaden their horizons by taking a gap year can benefit by bringing this wider outlook to their studies.'

So how do you go about it? It depends on if you know you want to defer when you apply to university. If you do, you can mark this on your UCAS application and include a statement showing the benefits of your R&D year, provided the course you're applying for allows deferment (most do). If you decide to defer after you've made your application, you can possibly still do so right up until quite late by speaking to the admissions tutor at your department. In most cases if you have a good reason they will be more than happy to allow it. Be warned: this varies by course, department and university so speak to your admissions tutor as soon as you've decided that an R&D year is for you. Don't delay.

WHAT COULD YOU DO ON AN R&D YEAR?

Although it's around 33,000 young people who defer their place at university to take a gap year, the actual number of those who take a year after school to experiment is much higher, with some sources like the National Youth Agency putting the figure at around 200,000. One of the nicest things about taking a year out is that there is no set path for what to do. The immense relief and freedom that many people feel when they realise this is probably a consequence of the fact that for nearly two decades they've been in a very structured environment, where each day they know precisely where they should be and what they should be doing.

Although we fully understand if you want to keep your R&D year free of structure and just see what happens, it's wise to have thought about some of the things that you want to achieve over the course of the year (or two years, or three – there's no saying that an R&D year has to be a fixed 365 days). That way you'll be able to enjoy the flexibility but still make the most of the experience. So what are these 200,000 young people actually doing with their time?

Career research

In the opening two chapters we revealed a process you can go through to make a fully-researched decision about what you want to do in the next phase of your life. If it's looking like you're not going to have the chance to fully explore that process while you're finishing school or college, then it makes sense to give over part of your R&D year to doing this research. Your R&D year could also be the perfect opportunity for you to arrange a few spells of work shadowing or work experience to allow you to do your real world research on what career is right for you. As well as that, if you want to do some travelling then you're probably going to have to earn some money – in which case you'll also need to get a job.

Work

If you're looking to get work – whether it's to save some money for your travels or just to see what it's like – the key is to have a strategy. Don't just get a job because it's local and pays well. Try to get a job in the industry or occupation that you'd potentially like to go into. Granted, it's unlikely that you'll find someone who will let you run a marketing department on a temporary contract, but if you join several good temp agencies (see Chapter 7 on getting a job) then you might be able to find a lower level role like data entry in the marketing department. As well as bringing in a wage from this vantage point you will be surrounded by the people doing the job you're interested in. You will get plenty of insight into what this is like as a career and some useful contacts – which can be more valuable than a salary.

Keep your mind open and don't make the mistake of thinking that you need to work in this country. In fact, there might well be more opportunities available to you if you expand your job search to include other countries. If you've always wanted to see the world, you might think that you have to split your gap year into the necessary elements of earning money and then spending it travelling. Not so. You could just as easily make your way to the other side of the world and work when you get there, allowing you to experience working culture overseas and travel at the same time.

There are thousands of jobs around the world that require seasonal labour and some which prize UK workers, such as teaching English abroad, fruit picking in Australia, chalet workers in the mountains and camp counsellors in the United States. Some recruitment agencies specialise in sourcing labour for these roles – so keep an eye out for these global opportunities.

REAL LIFE

I still think of myself as deferring from university, 15 years after leaving school. I still intend to do it one day, but I always said that if life got boring then I'd have uni as a back-up option. It's not got boring yet and any academic shortcomings I have were overridden by the experience I had at a young age.

Katie

Travel

Mark Twain (who is well worth reading more about, because he did more than just get quoted) said, 'Travel is fatal to prejudice, bigotry, and narrow-mindedness' and he's right. That said, you only need to see some of the Facebook updates from the people who return back from an R&D year threatening to educate you about the plight of an isolated tribe in some jungle to realise that travel can create its own problems.

Only kidding – it's true, travel does broaden the mind and allows you to get a sense of perspective about your own life. Just try to downplay this when you get back home – no one wants to see the videos you took, they're just being polite. Travel is often one of the most exciting parts of an R&D year. From the joys of planning a trip, selecting a travel partner (if you want one) and deciding on an itinerary, you can get almost as much enjoyment from travelling before you go.

Clearly, there are several things that you need to establish before you go off on your travels (see the 'Safe travelling' section later in this chapter). Your parents will probably insist that safety is near the top of that list, and although tragedies have befallen young travellers, planning properly can help you avoid many of the mistakes that can lead to accidents. Always bear in mind that you're much more likely to die from driving on UK roads than you are going on an R&D year – so if anything you're safer abroad...

Volunteer

Volunteering has always been popular with those on an R&D year. Given the fact that volunteering allows you to see another country and do your bit to help, it's a great thing to consider. Many schemes such as Raleigh International and organisations like Pathfinders Africa offer some incredible sounding packages, which could see you helping get water to a village, or saving exotic animals like mountain gorillas. What you choose to expend your energy on is entirely up to you – this goes back to the question posed in the opening chapter about what moti-vates you.

Many returning volunteers talk about the wonderful feeling you get from helping others. It's not all about the warm fuzzy feeling you get though – employers will always look at this sort of activity on a CV and be impressed by your thoughtfulness and dedication. Periods of volunteering can also help you with your research for what you want to do when you get back from your gap year. That said, don't think that just because you're volunteering that it will be free. You'll often have to pay many thousands of pounds to take part in the different schemes.

Study

It may seem strange to take a break from studying and then go and study, but there are plenty of courses both in the UK and abroad that you might fancy doing. These could be taster courses to see if you want to invest more time and money in studying the topic in more depth, or it could be something altogether different such as using the time to retake an A level or GCSE you feel you could have done better on.

R&D years are also an ideal time to look at doing a language course – after all, you couldn't get better practice than being immersed in a language and needing to concentrate on your lessons in order to be able to eat. Alternatively, you might just have a burning ambition to learn a particular skill – whether you've always wanted to go to Japan and learn karate or head to Italy to learn the secrets of making great pasta, the R&D year is your passport to those new skills.

Do nothing

Sitting around the house, playing on the computer, doing Sudoku puzzles, throwing playing cards into a bowler hat, eating kiwi fruit, learning to spell the name of that train station in Wales that ends in -gogogoch. Whatever it is that you do when you sit around with time to kill, you can schedule in plenty of this during your R&D year. Admittedly it's not the most productive use of time – and if you're still living at home then you can bet that your parents will point this out to you. But your defence as always should be that you're recuperating from two decades of constant education. You've earned a bit of time to sit around and do nothing.

TIP ✓

The Not Going To Uni perfect R&D year

Planning the perfect R&D year is fun. Just make sure that it's got elements of self-improvement and interest that will shine on your CV. Here's one example of a perfect year out:

○ Careers research and work shadowing on the shortlist of five careers.
○ Night classes and distance learning courses to learn Mandarin.
○ Working in a gym to get fit and earn extra money.
○ Volunteering at music festivals.
○ Volunteering for a charity at weekends to help out and get exposure to a particular role.
○ Three months' teaching English in China.
○ Three months' travelling back to the UK.

ACTION ⚡

Turn to the Notes section and see if you can plan a better year. Don't worry about costs for the time being, just make sure that it has a good balance between things you've always dreamed about doing and things that would develop your career opportunities. Next research some costs and see if you surprise yourself by how little it might cost.

HOW DO YOU AFFORD AN R&D YEAR?

This largely depends on what your plan is for the year. If you want 365 days of jetting around the world and staying in luxury hotels then you would be looking at tens of thousands of pounds. Not many people are after that though, so let's figure out a rough guide of how much it could cost for six months of travelling.

Note: this is working on a worst case scenario and is all approximate – you'll be able to shave hundreds (probably thousands) of pounds off this amount by shopping around and finding cheaper alternatives. For instance, you might prefer a European travel adventure for which you can get a train pass for €169.

- **Flights – £1000**. There are plenty of companies who will provide a multi-stop air ticket, which can be a great way of seeing several continents.
- **Living costs – £30 a day**. This is a huge cause of debate on travel forums as you'll find countries where you can eat and live like a king for £10 a day. It's no surprise that these tend to be the countries where you find lots of other backpackers.
- **Equipment – £500**. Everything from rucksacks to clothes and medicine.
- Total for a six-month period of travelling – **£6780**.

This may seem like a lot but when you factor in that you could spend six months earning £200 per week (currently the minimum wage is £4.98 per hour) that gives you £5200. If you live at home and keep your living costs very low over the six months, then you could spend the next six months having the time of your life. Beyond that it's a case of bringing to bear the commercial power of Christmas, birthdays and any trips to your relatives, selling anything you possibly can on eBay and taking all the extra shifts you can. You could also look at travelling for a shorter period. With hard work you'll get there, no matter where it is you want to be. So what are you waiting for?

SELLING YOUR R&D YEAR TO OTHERS

You might be on-board with the idea of an R&D year. You may be excited about the possibilities. That doesn't mean to say that everyone will be. Two main groups of people can hold you back at this point: friends and family.

- **Friends**. Why on earth would your friends not want you to take an R&D year? Quite simply, because they're jealous. By taking a year out you're doing something different and potentially something that's far more exciting than what they're choosing to do. Obviously, they could take one themselves but then it might be a bit further off the beaten track than they're prepared to adventure. They possibly haven't read this book and seen what a fantastic experience it could be. If you're feeling generous you could lend them the book when you're done.

- **Family**. Let's be honest, it's your parents who are the biggest source of criticism when it comes to your choice to take an R&D year, and given that they probably still exercise a good deal of control over what you do (imagine, for instance, if they took away rent-free/cheap living while you were saving up to go on your travels...) you need their buy-in. Your parents can say they object for all manner of reasons but behind it all is simple fear. Fear that you'll get bitten by a koala and develop rabies, or fear that you'll not live up to your full potential if you don't go to university.

In both of these situations the key to getting people on-side with your decision to take an R&D year is to calmly and patiently explain what's driving you to make this choice. The second you start to argue, the second you raise your voice, you've lost and it's always going to be an uphill struggle to convince them that you've thought about this rationally. If you know your own mind and can explain that then you won't have too many problems.

As an additional bonus you'll probably find that if people are behind you then they'll help you to achieve your goal. With your friends you can probably wait and see who it is that's feeling jealous (they'll be the ones who find a reason to criticise what you're doing). With your parents, though, it makes sense to emphasise that this is a mature, rational decision you're making by presenting it to them before they raise any objections.

Rather than just telling them that you're planning to take an R&D year and expecting them to deal with any concerns they have, consider asking for a meeting where you'll present your plans and answer their questions. It might sound like insanity to have a meeting with your parents but it gives you a great chance to present the idea properly. Write an agenda and make a PowerPoint presentation if it helps. Here are some of the things to cover:

○ Start by telling them that this isn't a gap year where you swan around the world and drink too much; it's an R&D year when you are investing time into making sure you have the best possible advantage for the years to come.

○ Explain that you are aware of the possible dangers and have researched the potential issues for the various countries that you're planning to go to with the Foreign & Commonwealth Office.

○ Explain that you are aware that although it theoretically puts you a year 'behind' everyone else who is off to university, you've seen several studies that say that employers these days are looking for a more rounded employee than someone who has only ever experienced school and university. Drop in that fans of deferment include the head of UCAS and that a recent YouGov poll said that 64 per cent of managers believe gap years would help to prepare a person for work – only 3 per cent felt that a degree was all someone needed to get a job.

○ You could mention that you feel the R&D year would be a brilliant time for you to do more research on your potential future careers and what would be the right path for you. Emphasise that with non-continuation rates at anywhere up to 28 per cent (depending on the university), clearly a lot of people are rushing into university and wasting their time and getting into massive debt – you don't want this to be you.

O Explain what you want to do. Tell them about the places you would love to see. Tell them about things you want to learn. Share your ultimate R&D year plan, let them see that it's not all sitting around throwing cards into bowler hats. Explain the volunteering projects that you would love to be involved in. Let them experience your enthusiasm and they'll be putty in your hands.

O Tell them you have a plan for saving up for the money and that any help would be gratefully received. (One idea would be to see if they would match the money you put towards your R&D year – even if it's £1 for every £10 you earn, it's worth a try!) Emphasise most clearly that you are not expecting them to pay for it.

O Finally, ask them if they have any other concerns or questions and although you don't know everything you'll do your best to find out their answers. Explain that although you know it's difficult you hope they can understand why you've made this decision and you hope they respect that. If you need an extra boost tell them that they could come and meet you on the other side of the world for a holiday.

REAL LIFE

My mum was petrified of me travelling but she preferred to offer incentives to do other things instead of just saying that she didn't want me to go away. So she said they'd pay for a car and let me live rent free if I went to university. It was a real pressure and I resented them not supporting me. I still went, but it would have been better if they could have understood why I wanted to take a year off.

Georgina

SAFE TRAVELLING

Let's be frank – people do die on their year out. That said, you absolutely have to defuse your own and others' concerns about travelling. If you are well prepared, you will face no greater dangers than you would do in the UK. It's fine to be cautious, just don't let that caution do anything other than spur you on to get well prepared – never let it hold you back. It sounds crazy but some people do. They get so terrified of all the awful things that they imagine *might* happen that they stay exactly where they are – in an environment that they feel safe in, simply because nothing bad has happened to them so far. They never quite become aware that wasting their one and only life is hands-down the most horrific thing that can happen to anyone.

There are really just four main things you need to do to ensure that your travels are safe – whether they're R&D year travels or any subsequent travelling you want to do.

1 Research

In terms of planning R&D travels you should always start at the Foreign & Commonwealth Office's website (www.fco.gov.uk). They have a campaign called Know Before You Go which gives plenty of good general advice, but it also gives the all-important country specific knowledge that you need. Each country is different and each will have small things that you might not have considered. For instance, as a Western woman you might never consider the requirement to cover your face or body, whereas in some countries it could cause significant problems if you went without a headscarf.

Knowing before you go is enough to defuse the problem, so get researching. Even if you're going abroad with a reputable company you should still make sure you research everything yourself as well. One of the important lessons travelling teaches you is to be responsible for your own well-being – you don't want to have a parent (or parent company) hovering over you your whole life, so start taking responsibility.

2 Equipment

The equipment that you pack should naturally depend on where you go. Equipment covers everything that you will need from the types of clothes, to the all-important requirements such as toilet paper, mosquito spray and so on. Your research will show you what you need to take, so speak to travellers who have been before and pay attention to their advice. Incidentally, one thing that nearly every traveller says is that they wish they'd brought more money and fewer clothes, so see if you can get the balance in your rucksack right. Other strange essentials include duct tape, plastic cable ties and Blu-Tack.

3 Medical

While you're researching, one of the things that you will need to look out for is if there are specific medical requirements for any of the areas that you're going to. Will you need to take anti-malaria medication? Are there any particular health threats in the country that you're going to? Is rabies an issue? All of these issues will be picked up in your research, so don't forget to act on them – this could conceivably save your life. The more straightforward aspect of this point is that you'll need to be fit to make the most of your travels. You're more likely to get out and see the amazing things around you if walking up a hill doesn't leave you gasping for breath and a Jaffa Cake.

4 Worst case scenario

It's a good rule for life to plan for what happens if things go wrong (see Tip box below). As the cliché runs – failing to prepare is preparing to fail. Outline some of the worst things that could happen and then construct reasonable plans for how you would get out of those situations. You'll find that the answer to several of the most common gap year problems is to have a good travel insurance policy. Insurance is so far beyond the realms of being an essential that if you even whisper the phrase R&D year you should be forced to buy it.

Whatever happens on your R&D year, it will be a defining time in your life that gives you space and (importantly) distance to think. Use the time wisely, enjoy every adventure that comes your way, including the bit where you work to earn the money to go. Don't forget to send us a postcard, but don't ask if we want to see your photos when you get back – we'll only get jealous (and bored).

ACTION

Get researching. Head onto the internet and find the forums and books that are recommended for the places you're interested in going to. As ever, don't just trust one source of information, look for three different viewpoints and compare them.

TIP ✔

Common gap year problems

Here are some of the most common gap year problems and how to avoid them:

- Lost passport/travel documents – take photocopies and colour photos of all your documents and save them to a Dropbox in the event that you lose your camera.
- Theft/mugged – if you are new to an area then you might find yourself wandering somewhere where mugging is a natural hazard. Try to get advice on safer areas and places to avoid and never advertise your possessions, even if you are insanely proud of your new digital camera.
- Injured – falling over skiing, bungee jumping injury, bitten by a snake. It's no wonder your parents were concerned. Travel insurance and an element of common sense is all you can have to protect yourself against this.
- Falling out with travel friends – this is practically a certainty. Plan for what to do when it happens and it will take the pressure off you when it does.
- Cancelled or delayed flights – just because you're going somewhere exotic doesn't mean that you can't get waylaid by the same things that hit normal travellers. Try to enjoy it. OK, so you're stuck in an airport but it's a probably much cooler airport on the other side of the world – how often does that happen?
- Running out of money – plan for how much you'll need before you go and have an emergency fund stashed with your parents in case you need it.

CHAPTER FOUR

HOW TO MAKE UNIVERSITY THE BEST INVESTMENT POSSIBLE

This Chapter in Brief

- We might be called Not Going To Uni, but we really do love students, lecturers and university in general.

- Honest.

- That said, university is a massive investment of time and money, so you have to be sure about your decision to do a degree.

- If you know university is right for you, then there are ways to reduce the costs.

- There are several different ways to get a degree that you might not even have heard about. Some are even free ...

It's annoying, but understandable, that when your organisation is called Not Going To Uni that people assume you somehow hate universities. Nothing could be further from the truth – we think university is an incredible system that gives some students academic and life experiences that they will benefit from for ever. We just think it makes sense when you leave school to have an awareness of every single option available to you. When schools and colleges are promoting university as the best option for every student it means we have to shout louder about the alternatives. Sometimes that means we get seen as being a touch anti-university and hand on heart, we're not. Honest.

So if you have researched all of your options – for instance, you're absolutely sure that working for a few years to get a better idea of what you like and *then* getting a degree isn't right or you know for sure you can't get professional qualifications instead – and you still feel university is right for you, then go for it. Just promise us one thing: before you press send on that UCAS application make sure you've read and understood the following statistics:

STATISTIC 1 – getting a degree could cost you over £50,000.

STATISTIC 2 – dropout rates for some universities are as high as 28 per cent.

STATISTIC 3 – unemployment six months after graduation is 10 per cent.

Of course, you can prove anything with statistics, so for balance let's have three good news statistics from university:

STATISTIC 1 – over the course of their careers, university graduates are likely to earn £100,000 more than those who leave school after their A levels – yay!

STATISTIC 2 – graduates are less likely to get depression than Level 2 educated students (for male graduates this is 55 per cent, female 35 per cent).

STATISTIC 3 – graduates are between 30 per cent and 40 per cent more likely to hold positive attitudes towards race and gender equality.

So, what's the point of all this statistical wondering? The point is quite simply that before you decide that university is right for you, you need to understand some of the finer points and make sure that if you choose to go to university you get the best deal possible. You need to be one of the people to experience the good side – where you do a well-respected course, minimise your debts and walk straight into a well-paying job; not the bad – where you pick the first course you find, rack up thousands of pounds of debt and credit card bills and struggle to find a job at the end of your course.

REAL LIFE

I'm still undecided about the value of my degree. I left with around £25,000 in debt but it was the £3000 in credit card debt that has proven the most difficult to deal with – it never dies! I did need a degree for my first job post university but it's taken me ten years at least to get back to grips with finances. I'd advise having a strict financial plan to deal with debt and sticking to it. I wish I had.

Andrew

HOW DO YOU PAY FOR UNIVERSITY?

With the recent increase in tuition fees, there has been a lot of discussion and debate about how students will even afford to pay for their studies in the first place. The fact is that although the government has more or less trebled tuition fees, there's actually very little financial outlay to go to university. You build up a portfolio of debt, rather than having to find £50k or so in hard cash.

TIP ✓

Note that this is the situation for England – Northern Irish, Welsh and Scottish universities have a slightly different system. See www.moneysavingexpert.com/students/student-loans-tuition-fees-change for more information.

When you are accepted onto a course you apply for a series of loans. These loans are delivered to your university to pay for your tuition fees and also to your bank account to pay for your accommodation and living costs (these are known as maintenance loans). The current plan is that you only start to repay these loans when you earn over £21,000. You then pay 9 per cent of your salary per month on anything you earn over that amount. So, for instance, if you earned £25,000, you'd be paying 9 per cent of £4000, or £360.

Be warned though: you will get charged interest on these loans, so while they sit there they are growing all the time. Not at a massive rate like you'd find if you borrowed this sort of money commercially (i.e. through a bank), but enough. So don't get the impression that in the early stages of your career you will have to suddenly find the money to repay your loans. However, the argument is that you're much more likely to get a job paying over £21,000 if you have a degree, so it balances out. You can debate that one yourself.

Let's have a look at the loans that are available:

Maximum tuition fee loans per year

Student type	Tuition fee loan
New full-time students	£9000
New full-time students at private university or college	£6000
New part-time students	£6750
New part-time students at private university or college	£4500

Source: directgov

Maximum maintenance loan rates for full-time students

Where you live and study	Maintenance loan
You live at home	£4375
You live away from home and study outside London	£5500
You live away from home and study in London	£7675
You spend a year of a UK course studying overseas	£6535

Source: directgov

On top of these maintenance and tuition fee loans there are what are called means-tested grants. These are dependent on your household income – so basically what your parents earn. If this is less than £25,000 then you could be eligible for the full grant of £3250 per year. Grants are allotted on a sliding scale, so providing your parents are earning less than £42,600 then you could be eligible for at least some grant, even if it's as little as £50.

These are the two main sources of income but you can also get help in other ways and these shouldn't be ignored:

1   Bursaries – most universities and colleges have a range of bursaries, which are grants that they pay out to students. These are given on a variety of different criteria from ethnic background to scholarly performance. You should speak to your university's finance department and ask for the details of their various bursaries.
2   Scholarships – if your family income is less than £25,000 per year then you could be eligible for help from the National Scholarship Programme. Each university has different criteria for what help will be available so check again with your chosen university's finance department.
3   Disabled Students' Allowances – there are grants available for those students who are on Disabled Students' Allowances (DSAs). Check what you could get if you think you qualify.
4   Students with dependants – if you have people you care for, either adults or children, then you could be eligible for grants.

5   Banks – most banks offer student accounts with interest-free or low interest overdraft arrangements. They will also offer you a range of credit cards. Be exceptionally careful of borrowing from banks and learn to calculate how much each piece of borrowing will cost you.

The changes to university funding have been radical and, as the protests witnessed in 2011 showed, have upset a lot of people. Clearly, the amount of debt that going to university forces you to build up is a massive pressure for many people and the early indications are that university applications for the 2011/12 academic year dropped by 8.7 per cent. That said, providing you do your research and make sure that the degree you're doing will enable you to get a job with a good salary at the end of it, then there's no doubt it's an investment worth making.

ACTION

In business, learning to cost out the different approaches you can take is a vital skill. Try it with your degree. Work out how much it will cost – not in vague terms but find the exact figure and write it out. Then cost out at least two alternatives – what other qualification paths could you choose and how much would they cost you? It's only by doing this that you can compare the relative values of your choices.

ARE AVERAGE GRADUATE SALARIES ACTUALLY TYPICAL?

There are conflicting reports about what graduates earn and clearly this can be a big factor in deciding whether or not to go to university, so it's worth seeing what some of the different earnings surveys reveal about typical graduate salaries. The different results come from how the different surveys calculate the earnings.

One of the major surveys is by the Association of Graduate Recruiters. It showed that in 2011 the average graduate salary would be £25,000. Clearly, this represents a good bet for graduates. They borrow heavily to get their degrees but then start on £25k, paying 9 per cent on the £4000 over the magic £21,000 mark. However, this survey is compiled by looking at what a number of very big companies are paying their graduate employees. These are typically large accountancy firms, legal companies and so on. In short, they are the sort of jobs where you would expect to see higher salaries.

Another survey that asked *all* graduates to report what they were earning suggested that the average earnings were just £19,695 (£22,228 in London). At this level you wouldn't be paying back your student loans, but they would be gaining interest and getting larger depending on the rate of inflation. Currently that's at around 5 per cent but this could go up or down – and that's another factor you have to take into account: take out student loans and you need to keep half an eye on what the country's financial rates are doing, just in case interest starts to get, well, interesting.

Your income per year	Interest rate on your loan
While you're studying	Rate of inflation plus 3 per cent
£21,000 or less	Rate of inflation
£21,000–41,000	Varies between the rate of inflation and the rate of inflation plus 3 per cent, depending on your income
£41,000 or more	Rate of inflation plus 3 per cent

Typical example

Let's take a typical example to see what could happen when you graduate. Let's say you take out the full range of loans for living and tuition in a degree outside London. You would have borrowed:

Tuition loans for three years: £27,000

Maintenance loans for three years: £16,500

While you were studying this would have risen at the rate of inflation (5 per cent) plus 3 per cent, so 8 per cent per year.

YEAR 1 –   8% of £14,500 = £1160

YEAR 2 – £14,500 + £1160 + £14,500 = £30,160

8% of £30,160 = £2412

YEAR 3 – £30,160 + £2412 + £14,500 = £47,072

8% of £47,072 = £3765

TOTAL OWED ON GRADUATION = £50,837

If after graduation you were to achieve an average graduate salary then you would earn £19,695. This would not be enough to start paying back your loans. However, the interest would continue to grow at the rate of inflation, which would mean that after a year of finishing university you would owe another £2541. Let's say you still haven't quite made the step up two years after graduation. That's another £2668 on the total – you now owe getting on for £60k. Keep an eye on the inflation rate (which can go up, don't forget) and make sure you don't lose your job.

Why are we making this point?

This is important because the changes in how students fund themselves through university mean that there is a significant risk. There are also significant rewards. However, the days of going to university just because you don't know what else to do or you want to mess around for a few years should officially be over. If you want some time without huge responsibilities then refer back to Chapter 3 and start planning your research and development year – it will give you all the time you need to think and relax and it won't leave you with an ever-increasing weight of debt to carry into your career.

Degrees are now the preserve of those who have properly researched their futures (see Chapters 1 and 2) and know that to pursue the career they want, then they absolutely need to get a degree because there is absolutely no other path available for them. For the record there are now fewer careers where this is the case. Degrees should also be reserved for those who have done a significant amount of homework on which university and course is most likely to help them achieve their goals. Because the other side of the growth in university funding is that you have to stop thinking like a school student and start thinking like a customer. If you're going to invest money in a degree then you have to shop around to see who provides the best value and return on your investment.

What about studying for the love of the subject?

Not everyone shares our view of university education. Some people still say that taking a degree simply because you love the subject, rather than because you can see how it will pay off, is an option. For the most part these are arts courses, where there is no concrete link between the subject and a job at the end of it. You might feel so strongly about a course that you're prepared to invest £50,000 in studying it with no clear job prospects at the end. We suspect you'll be in the minority.

Plus, think about it – if you really want to learn all there is about something like the history of art, for example, and you're prepared to spend £50k on it, ask yourself how many of the world's best galleries you can get to for that amount. The answer is all of them. You could then fund yourself to volunteer in a gallery for a couple of years, learn a few different languages while building up your working knowledge of the organisation and be the first on-hand when positions come up. Or you could get a degree.

This isn't a straightforward issue – you have to make your own decision about this question.

HOW DO YOU SHOP FOR A DEGREE?

There are two separate elements to consider when shopping for a degree:

O What course you choose.
O What university you choose.

To a certain extent the course that you choose will be determined by the fact that you go into your degree knowing what it is that you want to do afterwards. Don't just assume that all courses are the same because they've got the same name. You'll find that many employers have specific requirements about different degrees. Many HR departments will be happy to pass on advice about what sort of degrees they particularly look for. Take a look at some of the adverts for what you would consider your dream job – what are they asking for? Is it a named degree? Are there any other qualifications they want? You could also utilise the networks that you developed during your career research and ask what degree they would recommend. Again a mentor, if you chose to develop a mentor relationship, will have advice on this topic.

Beware of vague course choices. They often point towards the fact that you've not really done your career research thoroughly enough and you're hedging your bets that a general course will be enough to cover all your bases. Remember, degrees are no longer for people who are still making their mind up. Consider taking an R&D year and refining your choices further. While you're researching be sure to check that all the courses in your choice of subject cost the same. Although most universities charge the full £9000 tuition fees, some have started to cut costs to fill spaces.

When choosing your course you should take advantage of the open days, speak to previous students (who you can find quite easily through Facebook) and look at the course prospectuses. Don't forget these are advertising for the universities, so you need to read them with the full knowledge that they're trying to sell you something – they can skirt around their weaknesses. It shouldn't need to be said that you will have a very clear idea of what the course involves and how it matches your long-term career goals. If you don't understand an aspect of the course then speak to an admissions tutor or email one of the lecturers.

The second element of shopping for your degree is to look at the university. There are several competing things to assess here, all of which can make a massive difference to the sort of debts you're likely to graduate with.

- **Distance from home**. It's far cheaper to study closer to home, possibly with the idea of living at home while you study. Don't forget this often reduces the amount of money that you're entitled to in maintenance loans, but then it will also usually mean that you spend less on food and accommodation.
- **Sponsorships and bursaries**. There is a massive amount of difference in the sort of support that different universities give. One university might have a £10k bursary for students from your area, another might not charge fees for students called Jeff. It sounds stupid but the actual bursaries are often not much more sensible. It's your responsibility to research what bursaries are available and factor that into your decision.

○ **Facilities**. The universities are asking you to spend a huge amount of money – what do they give you to make that worth your while? What's the student union like? What sports facilities are there? A huge consideration is what the accommodation, libraries and IT facilities are like.

○ **Quality of product**. Despite the fact that most of the universities have rushed to take the chance to charge students the top fees allowable (it wasn't essential that they charged £9000 a year, but most universities decided to), not all of them provide a product of equal quality.

REAL LIFE

For me, being a live at home student really ruined the 'experience' side of going to uni. I get on with my parents but we all just had very different aims. If I wasn't studying they thought I should be working. I spent loads of time at friends' flats at uni and they were definitely having more fun. It was worth getting my degree but I'd advise anyone to think strongly about the sacrifice you make in seeing everyone else have fun.

Ric

The final point listed above might seem like the hardest to work out, but there are some league tables you can check out to see the quality of a university's product. The first is what's called the Research Assessment Exercise (or RAE). This is a score that's given to a department to say whether the work they do away from teaching students is particularly interesting or good. This affects the reputation of a university and how it is seen within industry – and consequently how their students are seen. Two other 'scores' worth noting are what they scored on the TQA (or Teaching Quality Assessment) and the NSS (National Student Survey).

Finally, it's well worth going back to your network of contacts and asking if any particular universities or courses are held in high regard for your potential career. This can sometimes give you slightly conflicting information as a course that used to be brilliant but is now falling behind might have a good reputation in the industry from the years when it produced good work. Combine the reputation with the scores and your personal requirements and you should be able to draw up a shortlist of universities that you're happy to visit.

GETTING THE MAXIMUM VALUE FROM YOUR UNIVERSITY EXPERIENCE

The main thing to note about extracting value from your course is to get the most out of it. This sounds like an obvious thing to say, but many students miss out on the extras that universities offer. Generalising wildly, but this is sometimes because they're focused more on the party experience of university rather than the other things that can make it valuable. Here are our top five things you should ensure you use:

1 **Partying**. Yes, we just said you shouldn't party too much but that's really because you shouldn't party exclusively and miss out on other things. However, university can be a brilliantly debauched and wild three years and if you miss out on that then you'll not have had the full university experience. Just remember the golden rule is to enjoy everything in moderation – including moderation.

2 **Careers services**. Most people forget about the careers office until their final year, and usually until the final semester of the final year. However, throughout your three years you can get some incredible opportunities through your careers service. The chance to meet employers, advice surgeries about interviews, CVs, contacts, the list goes on.

3 **Year in industry**. This is often an option for a range of courses, but you'll usually find that most courses will be able to find contacts in

industry to place you there. It's a great chance to develop an array of contacts and experience the job you'd like to do. You should also get paid a decent wage, which will go some way to helping you pay off your course fees.

4   **Alumni networks**. People often forget that these exist, but previous students (called alumni) are often available to current students as a pre-formed network to help you. These networks often extend into every profession and every company you can think of. If you're paying £50k for the privilege of wearing the 'old school tie' then you should certainly make it worth its while.

5   **Lecturers**. Departments these days live and die by their employability statistics. It's no longer enough that the courses are high quality and well-liked – if the graduates from a department are constantly failing to get work then no one will choose those courses. So lean on your lecturers. Ask for their contacts, ask for their advice, ask for work experience. Don't be rude about it but these guys owe you. After all, as Fats Domino once said, 'A lot of fellows nowadays have a B.A., M.D., or Ph.D. Unfortunately, they don't have a J.O.B.'

ALTERNATIVE WAYS TO GET A DEGREE THAT WILL BLOW YOUR MIND

You're probably aware of the phrase, 'There's more than one way to skin a cat.' Aside from making you wonder what sort of person came up with this phrase and whether the RSPCA got involved, it does make a valid point. If you've done the research and decided that the best way to achieve your chosen future goals is to get a degree, then so be it. But before you pack your bags and head off to university you should know that there are several different routes to getting a degree. You'll be pleased to hear that none of them requires sending money off to some dodgy 'e-university' from eBay.

Mindblowing university alternative 1 – sponsored degrees

Sponsored degrees can lead to you getting:

- O work experience
- O a degree
- O a job at the end of your degree
- O support for your resources (laptop, books, etc.)
- O paid!

That's right. There are sponsored degree programmes out there that will not only cover your costs, but also help you out with the essentials you need – and pay you while you're doing it. You're probably wondering how on earth you've not heard about sponsored degrees before. The truth is that they're still relatively new. The other factor is that they get a lot of applications for places and as such you'll probably find that companies don't have to push their sponsored courses all that hard – so there's no poster campaigns in the school careers' office.

You can find fuller details about sponsored degree programmes on the Not Going To Uni site, but some massive names in business run schemes such as KPMG, the Army, the Merchant Navy, American Express, Morrisons, Tesco and CapGemini.

ACTION

Go onto www.notgoingtouni.co.uk and see if there are sponsored degrees for the sort of courses that you would like to do. Even if it's not something you've given a thought to before, at least you'd know that you weren't missing out.

TIP ✓

Example of a typical sponsored degree programme

Logica offers a sponsored degree programme in association with the University of Winchester. It offers students the chance to study for free but also pays them a starting salary of £13,000 while studying for a BA (Hons) in Business Management.

On top of this, all your course materials are paid for, you get a laptop to work on and you are a Logica employee, so you get access to their benefits schemes and perks such as their home purchase plan, which is designed to help staff get onto the UK property ladder.

It almost seems needless to say but you get high-level experience working with one of the world's leading IT and business services companies. Students chosen for the course work with Logica for four days a week and attend university on the other day, so they still get a taste of university life.

THE NEGATIVES

You'll probably have realised that when something sounds too good to be true, that's usually because it is. Such is the case with sponsored degrees (or employer-funded study as it's sometimes called). The reality is that a company isn't going to pay for your degree for no reason – they want something back. In this case it's what they sometimes call 'golden handcuffs'. That means that you can get tied into a company after you graduate. In many cases it is a two-year period that you are obliged to work for the company, and if you leave before then you will become liable for the cost of the degree.

Another downside is that most of the companies will have you working for them during your degree time. That means you'll have to balance your study and your work. Granted, it will hopefully be the sort of work that's relevant to your course, so you'll get first-hand experience of the practical application of the theories you're learning. However, if your time management is poor (think back to revising for exams – were your timetables always messy and required you to do 22 hours of study in one day?) then this is the sort of thing that you might find challenging.

Finally, there's the thought that with the companies taking up a good deal of your time, what happens to your glorious three years of responsibility-free living? Who ever heard of a student who worked nine to five Monday to Thursday? Is that what you want? As ever, balance this against your desire to avoid £50k of debt, get some great experience along the way and the awareness that you can take many routes to different careers and futures, and you should come up with your own opinion on whether an employer-funded degree is right for you.

Mindblowing university alternative 2 – distance learning

If you thought that distance learning involved sitting at the back of the class then you're wrong, but you certainly wouldn't be the first to be surprised by this option. Essentially, distance learning involves doing a degree or other course *remotely*. So the course comes to you, in the form of emails, videos, dedicated websites, books, audio files and so on. You study in your own time and get assessed in a variety of different ways. The courses can be completed in three years but distance learning is more common as a part-time learning solution and so courses can be completed over an eight-year period.

PROPERTY OF MERTHYR
TYDFIL PUBLIC LIBRARIES

The most well known of the distance learning providers (and the biggest in the UK) is the Open University (OU). Although it has a physical campus in Milton Keynes, most of its students live all around the country and get their course materials sent to them. From here they can work through the curriculum at their own pace, fitting in their study at a time that suits them. Clearly, this has a lot of advantages for people who want to work as well as study. It's also ideal if you have adult or child caring responsibilities to balance with your desire to get on.

The other huge advantage for people taking distance learning courses is that they are often far cheaper than the university courses where you have to go to a university building. For instance, as we've already seen, if you paid for a BSc (Hons) Psychology degree at a university you would be looking at approximately £50k worth of investment. To do the same degree via distance learning with the OU would cost £5540, a tenth of the price! The Open University even has some courses that you can do for free, depending on your household income. So there are massive savings to be made.

Along with organisations specialising in degree and postgraduate studies, distance learning providers are often able to offer GCSEs, A and AS levels, and more. You can also study for a whole range of professional qualifications such as CIMA, ACCA, bookkeeping and sales. The chances are that whatever qualification you're looking at doing, someone somewhere will be offering a distance learning option for it.

THE NEGATIVES

One of the primary concerns people have about distance learning is whether the quality of teaching will be the same. In actual fact it's often just as good, with the course materials having been honed over hundreds of courses, so that it gives you a brilliant level of teaching. It's also a very modern way of approaching learning and gives students full exposure to many of the modern skills that employers look for, such as the ability to communicate and send and receive data via email and the web.

You might have to work a bit harder to explain to any future employers that your degree is just as valid. Clearly you could point out that it shows you have excellent internet and computer skills, you are able to motivate yourself and that you are able to balance the pressures of learning and working at the same time. In many ways you could argue that distance learning provides you with an even better preparation for the world of work – especially as 70 per cent of OU students work at the same time as studying, giving them priceless work experience as well as the all-important slip of paper and terrible graduation photo.

The fact remains that if you are the sort of person who could always find a reason to put off their homework then distance learning might not be for you. The motivation to see out the course has to come from you – and without your fellow students surrounding you (although you would have virtual access to them), would you be able to keep your interest going while work and other factors got in the way?

A short history of distance learning

Distance learning was a concept first pioneered nearly 300 years ago, by a man named Caleb Phillips of Boston, in the USA. In 1728 he launched a service that taught shorthand by correspondence over the mail, with each new class sometimes taking weeks to arrive! Naturally, distance learning has progressed to become faster paced.

The University of London was the first establishment to officially establish an external programme of distance learning degrees, in 1851. Nowadays, the vast majority of UK universities offer some form of distance learning while leaps in technology have allowed a new wave of educational opportunities that prove distance learning is no longer just available on television in the early hours.

Distance learning really has come a long way from its origins – the advent of the internet, in particular, has opened up higher education to many who would not have had the resources to pursue it otherwise. The University of London now has over 25,000 subscribers all over the world, and in the UK alone the Open University has a roster of students numbering more than 150,000. A good example of the breadth of courses on offer can be seen with the OU offering up to 580 courses in 14 different subject areas. The range of subjects on offer spans from mathematics to arts degrees and even subjects with a practical element, such as sciences. Despite some of the stereotypes about distance learning, 25,000 Open University students are under 25 years old.

Mindblowing university alternative 3 – studying abroad

When you mention international students, the picture that comes to mind is of overseas students coming to experience the UK higher education system. But international study is a door that swings both ways and many UK students, scared by the levels of debt that are part of the new UK university stereotype, are investigating what other countries' systems have that could benefit them. The main point to make about taking this option is that it will require a good deal of research. There are highly individual application processes that are distinct in each country, so it's not going to be a case of sending a form to UCAS and getting your place offered to you in a quick email.

However, for anyone prepared to put in the research there are several benefits, such as improved academic performance according to several studies, cheaper fees and the possibility of having some travel built into your degree experience. Thanks to membership of the EU, it's illegal for any country to charge a UK student a higher fee than they charge their home students, so with some research you'll find that there are several opportunities to get a degree while paying absolutely no tuition fees. For example, the cost of a degree in Finland, Iceland, Ireland, Norway and Sweden is precisely nil. Fees are very low in France, Italy, Spain and Germany. The plan is also that in coming years it will be possible to get student loans regardless of whether you choose to study in the UK or abroad, which will give you the best of both worlds.

REAL LIFE

I studied in Holland and it was amazing. The quality of British degrees seems to be largely based on the past – only recently there was a survey that said the quality of British teaching had dropped according to world standards. The university in Holland was modern, the students were approachable and I loved being the novelty student!

Peter

THE NEGATIVES

The primary reason that students often dismiss the idea of studying abroad is ignorance – as in they simply don't know that the opportunity to do it exists. Otherwise, why wouldn't students be queuing up for the chance to wander off either within the EU or across the world?

Clearly, the biggest barrier after not knowing about the opportunity is that it involves having a very different university experience from many of your friends. If you would rather fit in with everyone else and stay in your comfort zone then maybe studying abroad isn't for you.

The fact that you will be surrounded by people speaking another language (providing you don't go to university somewhere like America or Ireland) is either a positive or a negative, depending on your point of view. For some it could mean that they feel a greater sense of isolation, and homesickness becomes a problem. For others it could simply fuel the incredibly exotic feeling that they get from being on the other side of the world and equip them with a hugely valuable skill into the bargain. Again, this is a very personal choice and your research should take into account that the university experience will be different around the world.

There are a small number of sponsorships and bursaries available but these are few and far between and highly competitive. With the UK not yet having the ability to apply for UK student funding and study abroad, you might have to ask some searching questions about where you would find the money to pay for your living costs (providing your course was free or cheap).

Finally, one thing always to consider is how you think employers would view your decision to study abroad. The likelihood is that many of them would look at what you've done as a good example of taking initiative and finding a sensible solution to a problem like the high cost of UK education. You could also point towards your language skills as another excellent side effect of studying abroad. But there is a technical issue to bear in mind. The worst case scenario would be to train to be a doctor in another country, only to find that their courses are not recognised in the UK and you have wasted your time. So make sure your course counts when you get back to the UK, if indeed you want to come back! NARIC (http://www.naric.org.uk/) is a UK organisation that compares the educational merits of different courses from different countries and decides whether they are viable in the UK.

Mindblowing university alternative 4 – pimping your degree

What on earth is pimping your degree? Well, it's the term we coined for all the changes and tweaks you can make to a standard degree course to make it more affordable. Universities are acutely aware that rising costs are making courses much more difficult for students to afford, so they've got several different versions of degrees available that can make them more attractive.

FOUNDATION DEGREES

Foundation degrees are two-year courses where you work with a company to study a particular subject and learn about it at university. It works in much the same way as an apprenticeship, where you study in an academic environment (either a university or a higher education college) and also learn about the job within a company.

At the end of the two years (longer if you do it part-time) you will have a foundation degree qualification which you can then extend to a full degree, or simply take your skills and experience into the workplace. An example of this type of degree would be that offered by Tesco, which helped to shape a foundation degree for the retail sector. As a result students can now learn about retail at university or a higher education college at the same time as gaining experience of working life with one of the world's biggest retailers.

FAST-TRACK DEGREES

The idea of a fast-track degree (also sometimes known as a condensed degree) is that it takes a normal three-year course and squeezes it into two years, thus giving you a 33 per cent discount on both living expenses and tuition fees. Currently the number of fast-track courses is limited but they have been a popular addition and it's expected that the number will rise with demand.

STUDYING NEAR HOME

One of the simplest ways to cut costs for your degree is to choose the closest university to your home. This means that you can live at home and commute to lectures. Clearly, this relies on the fact that your parents wouldn't charge you rent and it means that you are pretty much stuck with whatever courses a university near you has to offer. If they happen to offer a well-respected course in your chosen field then this could be an option for you. However, it would be a false economy to think that just because you can save several thousand pounds from the cost of university that it would be good value if you ended up with a degree that didn't open an employer's doors.

THE NEGATIVES

With any changes that you make to a standard length degree, there will be downsides. Studying close to home might mean that you save on accommodation costs but it could seriously restrict the social side of the experience; likewise doing a fast-track degree could speed things up but it could leave employers wondering if you got the same depth of learning experience. Always bear in mind that you might end up needing to explain (and justify) the decisions that you've made, possibly to an employer. As always though, if you can make a solid argument and put across the reasons why you made the decisions that you did then you can only enhance your reputation.

Grow and Develop your Career

Fusion People Training
has a unique blend of
training expertise, employer
relationships and recruitment
and placement knowledge.

Call: **0207 653 1078**
Visit: **www.fusionpeopletraining.com**

Apprenticeships   City& Guilds   edexcel   ncfe

CHAPTER FIVE

EVERYBODY LOVES APPRENTICESHIPS

This chapter in brief

- ◯ Forget everything you thought you knew about apprenticeships.

- ◯ One important thing to know is that they're free if you're under 19.

- ◯ You can earn while you learn and they're available in almost every subject imaginable.

- ◯ You end up with qualifications, work experience and no debts.

- ◯ Even if a company doesn't do an apprenticeship, you can convince them to start a scheme.

If you really want to know how good apprenticeships are, here's a statistic that will blow your mind. The latest figures show that in 2010/11 over 440,000 apprenticeships were started. The number has doubled between 2006 and 2011. If people are choosing to avoid university to escape the debt then it seems fairly clear about where they are heading instead. The other stunning thing to know about apprenticeships is that it's not just 16–18 year olds who are taking them. Over 300,000 of the apprenticeships that were started were taken by those over the age of 19 (known as adult apprentices).

There's evidence to suggest that one of the groups desperate for apprenticeships now is none other than university graduates, who see the apprenticeship as the perfect way to get into employment. So, people are leaving school, spending £50k on a degree and finding that what they actually need to get into a job is an apprenticeship. So, um, why not just do the apprenticeship, and if you find that you need a degree afterwards then do that? It's easy to progress an apprenticeship into a degree once it's finished. Sounds good, doesn't it? One possible reason that people are dismissing apprenticeships without considering them is that they've bought into the myths surrounding apprenticeships.

TIP ✓

Myths about apprenticeships

○ They're only available for plumbers. Nothing could be further from the truth. Apprenticeships are available in over 200 industries from cutting edge technology to hands-on agriculture.

○ You don't get paid. You do. There's a minimum wage for apprentices (currently £2.60 per hour) and the majority of apprentices get paid far more than that per week.

- You don't get a job at the end of it. While there's no guarantee that you'll get a job with the company you do your apprenticeship with, over 90 per cent of apprentices are entering work or education after their apprenticeship.
- The qualification isn't as good as a degree. It's a different type of qualification, which means it has different strengths and weaknesses. Plus you can always pursue your qualifications after the apprenticeship, even progressing to a full degree.
- They are done by people who aren't sure what to do. Ninety-three per cent of people complete their apprenticeships – it doesn't sound like people who don't know what to do, does it?
- They're about employers taking advantage of young people. In some sectors up to 89.5 per cent of companies were still employing their apprentices five years after they'd finished their apprenticeship (as real employees!).
- They cost a fortune! Not at all, in fact if you're aged between 16 and 18 then your training is completely free. If you're between 19 and 24 then you'll pay 50 per cent of your course fees. Older than that and it depends on the industry and employer you're applying to.

One of the biggest things that holds back the idea of going for an apprenticeship is one of snobbery. To some people (people who might be your parents and teachers) an apprenticeship somehow seems a *lesser* sort of qualification than a degree. What's absolutely, 100 per cent bonkers is that this attitude is based on out-of-date information. In exactly the same way that we might have to shout at our grandparents for having out-of-date attitudes towards other cultures, so we should shout at anyone who screws up their noses at the idea of getting an apprenticeship, because they're just for plumbers. Tell them that they get you into work, pay you to learn and give you instant access to a network of employers: they're amazing!

If this is the first time you've considered (or even heard of) apprentice-ships then let's start at the beginning. Scientists think that the Big Bang was caused by...wait, that's a bit too far back, let's skip forward a bit...

WHAT IS AN APPRENTICESHIP?

An apprenticeship is a period of training lasting anywhere up to four years, where you split your time between an employer and a training pro-vider. Historically, companies took on an apprentice when they wanted to train up a new employee and it was considered to be the best way to get into different occupations. In modern times an apprenticeship works in any career where you can learn best by a combination of on- and off-the-job training. When you think about it, that's pretty much every job, which is why you find apprenticeships in so many different fields.

REAL LIFE

We took on two apprentices because we were sick of employing people who weren't really interested in working in an engineering firm – because there was training involved it seemed to generate a better response of candidates who had thought more deeply about the industry. We've since employed both of the first apprentices and we're running another scheme.

Alan

One of the unique things about apprenticeships is that you are helped by both an employer and a training provider. Because you are recruited by a company it means that you are a fully paid-up employee, which ensures you get paid and receive all the other benefits that employees get, like holidays. However, you also have that period of time (often one day per week or fortnight) outside the company when you study a related subject with a training provider. Your training provider could be any college or company that gives you the technical side of the training that you need to get good in a job. The company should treat you like a normal employee and put you to work doing the job you're paid to do. That said, they will give you support.

The qualifications that you get to do are vocational qualifications such as NVQs, BTECs or City & Guilds (see Chapter 6) and relate to the job you are doing. One of the great things about an apprenticeship is that it enables you to mix learning styles. There are the times when you are at work actually doing the job that you're paid for, then there's the time with your training provider when you learn more about the theory of the job. Apprenticeships are designed with employers, so they offer a structured training that enables you to learn the exact skills you need to do a job well. You'll also get targets to ensure you're progressing and that your employer is giving you the right support.

It's not just young people who value apprenticeships. Employers are wild about them too, because they provide a way to get new employees into their business, with lower costs. It also means that they can share the training burden and get support themselves on how to develop you as a member of staff. You can probably see why so many apprentices end up being recruited by their employer after the apprenticeship ends – largely because they've been custom-trained to be the sort of employee a company wants.

Another reason the companies like them is because apprentices are exposed to the latest techniques and training. Many employers report that having an apprentice is a very useful learning process for them as well. Imagine if you've been working in an industry for several years – you might not have had the chance to keep up with all the new ways of doing something. An apprentice gives the employer a chance to see how things are being done at the cutting edge.

TIP ✓

They're not just for plumbers!

There are over 1200 different roles where you can get an apprenticeship. That accounts for nearly every single occupation that you can possibly think of. Over 100,000 employers in 160,000 different workplaces offer apprenticeships, which means that wherever you are in the country and whatever you want to do an apprenticeship in then you will be able to find a scheme that you can do (and if you can't, see the section on creating your own apprenticeship later).

To give you a taste of the sort of different areas in which you can do an apprenticeship, here are some of the eye-opening ones we've seen recently:

- IT support
- Sport
- Marketing
- Search engine optimisation
- Plumbing (OK, so it is for plumbers as well!)
- Hotel receptionist
- Chef
- Mechanical engineering
- Beauty therapy
- Accounting
- Child care
- Elderly care
- Animal care
- Legal executive
- Horse jockey
- Video production
- Warehousing
- Furniture design
- Media communications
- Recruitment

Michael Jones

Engineer Training Programme with National Grid

Having completed a degree at University and feeling that nothing could top the experience and fun I joined the world of unemployment. Struggling with part time jobs while looking for that dream role, getting my hopes up with an interview to be told I lacked experience. It's different to what you are led to believe, that a degree guarantees you a better paid job, well I was struggling to find one!

Late summer 2009 I stumbled upon National Grid's vacancies for their Engineer Training Programme (ETP). A level entry requirements and offering a great salary, benefits and fully paid degree, I sat wishing I'd seen this sooner!

This job had it all; it seemed too good to be true, company car, paid degree, balance between learning and experience, as well as a guaranteed job with National Grid.

Two years on, I've nearly completed a second degree at one of the most highly regarded engineering Universities in the UK. This time with no student debt or worries about the cost of food or accommodation and completing it with a bunch of colleagues who will be friends for life.

The other half of my time is spent on site gaining valuable experience as a Substation Engineer. My mentor helps to put all that theory into practice and that's when things start to fall into place. The training facilities are great with fully qualified staff they really make learning a breeze.

I've also been on several self improvement courses, like the team building exercise in Cumbria with Outward Bound, learning new life skills like building a rescue bridge. (Shown above climbing to the top of Great Gable).

I consider myself blessed to have had this opportunity. I don't regret going to University but the Engineer Training Programmes is a great alternative and I believe it offers much more than just a qualification. It 's a job for life.

For more information visit
www.nationalgrid.com

ACTION

Take a look at the 1600+ different apprenticeships on www. notgoingtouni.co.uk and see if there are any in the sort of work you'd like to do.

WARNING – NOT ALL APPRENTICESHIPS ARE THE SAME

Just as you'll be aware that not every degree from different universities is the same thing, or indeed the same quality, so it is that not every apprenticeship is the same. There is a lot of discussion at the moment as to what the term 'apprenticeship' should be allowed to apply – some of the courses that are currently advertised are much shorter than others, so is it right that two people could spend different lengths of time on a scheme and both be considered as having done an apprenticeship? Not at all.

The simplest way of judging the merits of an apprenticeship is to see what concrete things it offers and how that fits with your requirements (salary/ benefits/qualifications). Make sure you look at the qualifications framework in Chapter 6 to understand the level of qualification (i.e. how advanced it is) an apprenticeship is offering. You might be adamant that you want an apprenticeship that offers a particular type of qualification, or it could be that it gives you experience in a particular field – the only person who can compare different apprenticeships and see which one is best for you, is you. Generally speaking there are three different levels of apprenticeship:

1   Intermediate – a level 2 qualification
2   Advanced – a level 3 qualification
3   Higher – a level 4 qualification.

For comparison:

○ GCSE grades D–G would be considered a level 1 qualification.
○ A full degree would be considered a level 6 qualification.

For a full comparison of different qualifications take a look at the chart in Chapter 6.

WHY BOTHER WITH AN APPRENTICESHIP?

What and how you learn in your apprenticeship will vary, but from a career point of view you'll definitely end up with the following:

○ Practical experience, skills and knowledge for working in your industry.
○ Functional Skills qualifications, e.g. English, maths and ICT.
○ A technical certificate such as a BTEC or a City & Guilds.
○ A work-based qualification, e.g. a National Vocational Qualification (NVQ).
○ Any extra qualifications important for your chosen occupation, such as a health and hygiene certificate.

Getting on in life is just one side of the deal though – you'll also receive some more immediate benefits. The following are three of the best.

1 Money

The deal with apprenticeships is that you earn a good wage while you continue to learn. If you're entering the world of work for the first time, you'll start earning a wage from the very beginning of your apprenticeship. According to research from the TUC, the average salary for an apprentice across all the different subjects and levels was £12,634. The key thing to remember with this though is that your salary will vary depending on what line of work you're in. Just as in the working world, some jobs command better salaries than others. Here are some other things that affected the salary rate, according to the TUC's research:

- Large companies pay better. The average salary for large companies was £14,059.
- 14.5 per cent of companies paid their apprentices bonuses worth on average £2039.
- The highest average salaries were paid by companies in the 'transport: shipping and ports' category of industry and were at the rate of £18,240 per year.
- The lowest rates were £10,433 and were in education.
- As an apprentice's skills develop and they begin to progress, their pay will increase accordingly.

Perhaps the most important earnings information of all came from a recent report called 'First Steps To Wealth', which showed how much people were likely to earn over their careers based on what qualification they got. The report showed the following:

- An average graduate should earn £1,611,551 over a working career of 45 years.
- An average 18 year old going straight to work should earn £1,023,840 over a 48-year career span.
- An average 16 year old going straight to work should earn £783,964 over a 49.5-year career span.
- Some apprentices (depending on subject) can expect to earn £1,503,726 over the course of their career.

Looking at these statistics it should be clear to see just how valuable it can be to invest in your future with some extra training. Just think, it could take you as little as a couple of years to get an apprenticeship, you'd get no debt and over the course of your life you'd earn around half a million pounds more than someone who didn't bother. Are they crazy?

2 Evidence of your abilities and reliability

When you've done your apprenticeship, you'll have a set of nationally recognised qualifications. Either you can use these to enhance your chances of employment with the employer you did your apprenticeship with, or you can take them to the labour market (i.e. go and get another job) and see if it makes other employers interested in you.

You must never underestimate the value of the experience that you've gained either. Although it's not as tangible as a certificate, to most employers the fact that you've spent a few years turning up for work every day and proving that you can develop yourself and pass exams will make you a much safer bet for employment than someone without that evidence.

The other thing that you'll have (if you're leaving the employer you did your apprenticeship with) is a reference. Again this is invaluable to future employers, so always try to leave a company on good terms. Even if you've been desperate to tell the boss what you really think of them, it's almost never a good idea if it means you won't get a good reference.

3 Benefits

Like most employees, you will be given paid holiday. Your individual entitlement will be detailed in your training agreement: 20 days is an average holiday entitlement. You'll probably get bank holidays as well, which means you can look forward to some long weekends. You may also be able to take some time off for study leave, in addition to your usual paid leave.

Many employers also offer opportunities to get involved in out-of-work activities, including social events, community projects or volunteer programmes. Make the absolute most of these opportunities as they can all help to develop your contacts and range of experiences or skills. Your employer should also ensure that you have a mentor. Their job is to make sure that your training fits your personal requirements, offers the skills needed for the job and meets required standards. They will also be there to help you through any difficult times and answer any questions you may have.

REAL LIFE

I still have to explain to mates who've gone to uni that I get paid on my holidays. They're spending a fortune on getting qualifications and then have to work during holidays to take the edge off the debt – I'm off to Benidorm for a week!

Steven

HOW DO YOU GET AN APPRENTICESHIP?

If you've decided that an apprenticeship is right for you, all that remains is to actually get the one you want. A word of warning: you have to realise that competition for places on popular schemes can be ferocious – you're not the only one to have realised what a good thing these apprenticeships are! You have to be serious in how you approach getting an apprenticeship. Don't expect anything to be handed to you and realise that you are entering the world of work, where professional appearance and conduct is essential.

There are just three steps to finding and securing the perfect apprenticeship:

Step one – decide what you'd like to do

Step two – find the opportunities

Step three – get the apprenticeship.

Step one – decide what you'd like to do

There's no escaping it, you need to get involved with Chapters 1 and 2. Just because you're not going to accumulate much debt doing an apprenticeship, that doesn't mean you can just close your eyes and stick your finger in a college prospectus. You need to be certain that the course you will invest your time and energy into is the right one for you. So get a pen, turn back to Chapter 1 and begin the process of discovering a future career that will make you excited. Trust us, it's not as painful as you're imagining it might be.

Step two – find the opportunities

Let's assume there's just been one of those swirly things they do in films to show that time has passed and you've now done your research and picked a career you're head over heels in love with. Now you have to find an apprenticeship in the right area of the country. This might not be an easy task and you'll probably know from thinking about your own home town that specific industries tend to gather together in different areas of the country. However, with time and effort you should be able to track down a job near you that will make the perfect apprenticeship.

To start your search and help get your placement you should closely examine all of the following five resources. Note the bonus mystery option at the end as well.

1   **Notgoingtouni** – http://www.notgoingtouni.co.uk/jobs. We've got thousands of apprenticeships and placements on the site and you can search geographically as well as by sector to help you pin down the best apprenticeship for you.

2   **Apprenticeships** – http://www.apprenticeships.org.uk/. The government's Apprenticeship Matching Service offers a lot of different advice and apprenticeships for you to browse.

3   **Local job centre** – http://jobseekers.direct.gov.uk/. A visit to your local job centre will give you a good insight into the sorts of industries that are hiring near you. Even if they don't offer an apprenticeship scheme you will be able to identify where the opportunities are.

4   **Local papers**. Companies often advertise their apprenticeship vacancies in the local paper and if you're quick then this can be a good place to spot a good position.

5   **Local colleges and training providers**. Your local college will have contacts with local companies that are looking to create apprenticeships and they will offer these to students. Speak to them about what they have available and they will be able to put you in touch with the companies, as well as advise you on the sort of qualifications you will get.

6   **Bonus mystery option (See tip box below)**.

Step three – get the apprenticeship

Remember: you're not automatically guaranteed an apprenticeship place. Competition is getting fiercer all the time for apprenticeships so you need to be diligent in how you apply to stand the best chance of getting a position. It's exactly the same as applying for a job – you'll have to convince people to take you on by showing them you're the best candidate. You'll have to present yourself well, 'sell' yourself and show them that you're the right person for the job.

The application routes for apprenticeships are more or less the same as when you're applying for a job in that you'll need to respond to the advert, either with a covering letter (which explains why you're the right person for the role) or with a CV. Sometimes they'll ask for both. Alternatively the company may use an application form. Take a look at Chapter 7 for a full rundown on how to get a job and the ways to make sure you ace the application, as well as how to cruise through any interviews or assessments the company wants to do. Don't panic: it might sound like a very challenging thing to do but once you've learned how it works, it's actually easy and can even be fun.

TIP ✓

Convincing companies to set up apprenticeships

A relatively common scenario among people searching for an apprenticeship is that they end up finding a company that sounds amazing but the organisation don't offer an apprenticeship scheme. Although there are over 160,000 workplaces that do have them, that still leaves a lot of companies who are yet to see the benefits of starting their own scheme. If this is the situation that you're in then there is a (slightly cheeky) tactic you can try: convince the company to start up their own scheme.

Clearly, asking a company to start an apprenticeship scheme requires a fair amount of confidence, so make sure you've done all of your research before you get in touch with them. Ideally you'll want to speak to someone high up in the company – the owner, managing director, or alternatively someone who works in human resources. The idea is to explain your situation and ask them if they would consider starting an apprenticeship scheme.

Key to this approach is selling the benefits to the business. Fortunately there are plenty! With research you could find some more specific benefits for a particular company, but here are some angles to investigate:

- Do any of the company's competitors offer an apprenticeship scheme? Companies hate being left behind their competitors.
- 80 per cent of consumers would rather do business with a company that has an apprenticeship scheme, so it's a good way to attract customers.
- There are a number of schemes offered by the government which can offset the costs, such as direct financial assistance – for example, the new £1500 grants per apprentice.
- There is no obligation to pay for apprentices' training (depending on age).

Above all, they would get a hugely enthusiastic, low-cost employee who would bring cutting-edge techniques and knowledge into the organisation. As with all speculative applications (what it's called when you apply for something that doesn't necessarily exist), it's key to have a good rapport with whoever you are communicating with – you are giving them first-hand experience of why you're so marvellous that they should bend the rules for you.

Never be in doubt: every company in the world will make room for someone who impresses them. It's a tougher option than just sending off your CV for an apprenticeship you like the sound of, but never assume that just because you can't see an obvious entrance, there's not a way in. That's what everyone else will assume, but the fact that you know differently gives you a huge advantage.

REAL LIFE

I've got about two months left on my apprenticeship at a company where there was never a scheme before I suggested one. Fortunately, I had a really good tutor who had contacts and they were able to support me in suggesting they start a scheme. Once the boss saw that it was a good deal for them as well, it was really easy. I love the job and have learned loads.

Shanelle

nationalgrid

Help us keep everyone connected.

Engineer Training Programme

This is a call to college leavers, graduates or career changers.
This programme is the complete deal and the real alternative to going to University.
It's an opportunity not to be missed!

Not only do we offer you a permanent position from day one with a starting salary of £23,500 but we also pay for you to study a foundation degree at Aston University worth around £30,000, plus a new car to support with the travel during training, accommodation and expenses. There really isn't anything more we could offer you to start building your career as a technical problem solver in engineering.

So if you are one of those people who learn through doing then this practical course is for you. There is a great support network available to make your journey successful.

On completion, not only will you be debt free (no university fees), but you will have secured a degree in either Electrical Power Engineering

or Gas Transmission Engineering and be moving onto a salary of £30,150 per annum.

Every year we have in the region of 70 positions available for the Engineer Training Programme across approximately 42 locations nationwide. Recruiting people from their local communities is important to us so that you are supported from home as well as work. We have a few remaining vacancies available for this year to start with us in September 2012 but we will be starting our 2013 recruitment campaign from September 2012 as well.

Minimum entrance requirements are two A2 Levels in either Maths, Physics or Engineering (A-C Grade) or a HNC, HND, BTEC, ONC or degree in an engineering related subject.

Take action today and apply at
**www.nationalgridcareers.com/
Development-Opportunities**

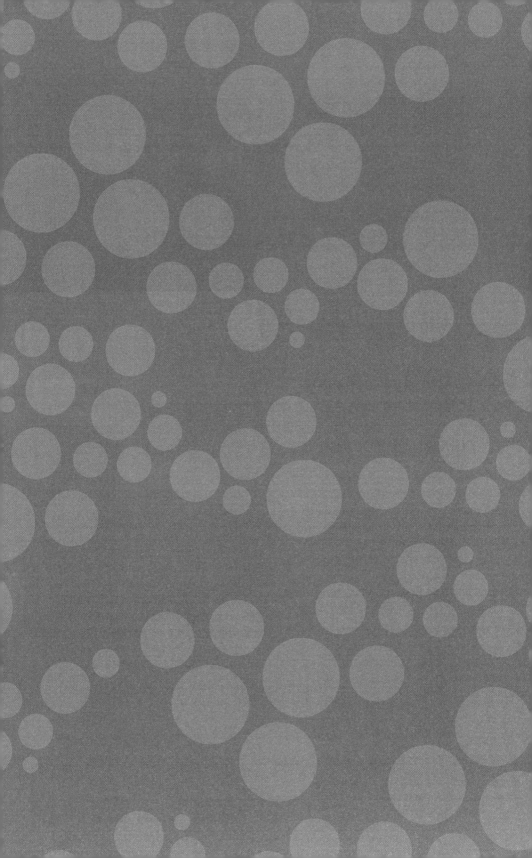

CHAPTER SIX

VOCATIONAL QUALIFICATIONS

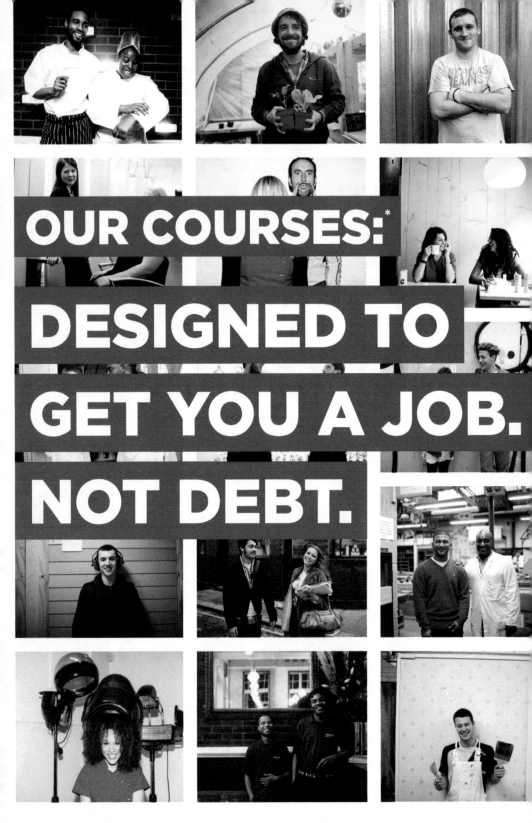

OUR COURSES:*
DESIGNED TO
GET YOU A JOB.
NOT DEBT.

*Our courses go to Level 7, which is equivalent to a Masters degree.

City&Guilds

Believe you can

Find the course you need near you: www.cityandguilds.com

This chapter in brief

- ○ Vocational qualifications are a more practical, hands-on form of training that you do if you want to show an employer you can do a specific job.

- ○ The best way to compare different qualifications is through a framework, which ranks the different courses.

- ○ There are a huge range of different qualifications, all with their own merits.

- ○ Some vocational qualifications are as demanding as a postgraduate degree.

- ○ Study for vocational qualifications is often with employers or further education (FE) colleges, but increasingly universities are offering vocational courses.

Let's assume for a second that you never received a full and frank appraisal of your options for after you leave school. Let's go one step further and assume that all of the information that you did receive was somewhat pro-university. If that's the case for you then we have an introduction to make: please meet vocational qualifications, you might just like each other. We'll come to explain exactly what vocational qualifications are in a moment but first let's take a second to try to unravel the complexities of the various strands of qualifications available to you.

We apologise if you are about to experience your first government jargon speak induced headache (or GJSIH if you'd rather) but it's useful stuff to know. It's useful because it allows you to see how all the different qualifications (not just vocational) compare. That way if a course is offering a BTEC Professional Diploma and another is promising an A level, you'll be able to see which is the more advanced. That way you can make sure that you're taking a course at a level you feel comfortable with and get the best option for you.

First of all the qualification strand you'll probably be most aware of is the Framework for Higher Education Qualifications (or FHEQ). This consists of the degrees (Honours, Masters and Doctoral) that everyone is aware of, although perhaps you might not have known that beyond an Honours degree (a standard university degree) lies the qualifications of Masters and Doctoral level. The latter is most often referred to as a Doctor of Philosophy, or a PhD – even if the subject has nothing to do with Philosophy, told you it was crazy!

The second framework is the National Qualifications Framework (NQF). This is put together by the regulators in England, Wales and Northern Ireland. The three regulators all meet and agree on the different levels of qualification and which level they should be placed in. In this way it ensures that all of the qualifications that are included are of a good enough quality. It also means that they'll be recognised on a wider basis.

The final qualification framework is the Qualifications and Credit Framework (QCF). This is used exclusively for vocational qualifications. So if you want to compare which vocational qualifications are the most advanced then take a look at the QCF.

REAL LIFE

As an HR officer I know plenty of employers who struggle with this issue of what qualifications are valuable. Once you've not been in education for a few years it's very easy to lose track of what qualifications are out there. If you want my advice, only pick the ones with a recognisable 'brand' name attached to them and accept that most employers will think that the exams were harder in their day – you'll probably think the same when you're older!

Helen

Now although this sounds like gobbledegook, it is useful because if you take a glimpse at the table below then you'll see once and for all that regardless of what sort of education you pick, you can keep on progressing through the different levels to reach the top. You can also see by glimpsing across the table that although the qualifications might be pursued in slightly different ways, and taught using different methods and involving employers to a greater or lesser extent, no one qualification strand is *better* than the others. If you want to do a degree, that's fine – but it's no better or worse than holding a BTEC Advanced Professional Diploma. If you want to get some A levels, then that's great – but you can't consider yourself *more qualified* than someone with an NVQ at level 3.

Level	National Qualifications Framework (NQF)	Qualifications and Credit Framework (QCF)	Framework for Higher Education Qualifications (FHEQ)
Entry	O Entry level certificates O English for Speakers of Other Languages (ESOL) O Skills for Life O Functional Skills at entry level (English, maths and ICT)	O Awards, Certificates and Diplomas at entry level O Foundation Learning at entry level O Functional Skills at entry level	
1	O GCSEs grades D–G O BTEC Introductory Diplomas and Certificates O OCR Nationals O Key Skills at level 1 O Skills for Life O Functional Skills at level 1	O BTEC Awards, Certificates and Diplomas at level 1 O Functional Skills at level 1 O Foundation Learning Tier pathways O NVQs at level 1	
2	O GCSEs grades A*-C O Key Skills at level 2 O Skills for Life O Functional Skills at level 2	O BTEC Awards, Certificates and Diplomas at level 2 O Functional Skills at level 2 O OCR Nationals O NVQs at level 2	
3	O A levels O GCE in applied subjects O International Baccalaureate O Key Skills at level 3	O BTEC Awards, Certificates and Diplomas at level 3 O BTEC Nationals O OCR Nationals O NVQs at level 3	

Level	National Qualifications Framework (NQF)	Qualifications and Credit Framework (QCF)	Framework for Higher Education Qualifications (FHEQ)
4	O Certificates of Higher Education	O BTEC Professional Diplomas, Certificates and Awards O HNCs O NVQs at level 4	O Certificates of higher education O Higher national certificates
5	O HNCs and HNDs O Other higher diplomas	O HNDs O BTEC Professional Diplomas, Certificates and Awards	O Diplomas of higher education O Foundation Degrees O Higher national diplomas
6	O National Diploma in Professional Production Skills O BTEC Advanced Professional Diplomas, Certificates and Awards	O BTEC Advanced Professional Diplomas, Certificates and Awards	O Bachelors degrees O Bachelors degrees with honours O Graduate certificates and diplomas O Professional Graduate Certificate in Education
7	O Diploma in Translation O BTEC Advanced Professional Diplomas, Certificates and Awards	O BTEC Advanced Professional Diplomas, Certificates and Awards O NVQs at level 5 (in the QCF framework)	O Masters degrees O Integrated masters degrees O Postgraduate certificates O Postgraduate diplomas

Level	National Qualifications Framework (NQF)	Qualifications and Credit Framework (QCF)	Framework for Higher Education Qualifications (FHEQ)
8	O Specialist awards	O Award, Certificate and Diploma in strategic direction	O Doctoral degrees

Source: Direct.gov.uk

Warning #1: These levels are corresponding to each other but they clearly place a different emphasis on the styles of learning, so just because it's possible to get one level of qualification under one of the frameworks, doesn't necessarily mean that you could automatically pass the same level under a different framework. Also the FHEQ only broadly corresponds to the other frameworks, but it's still useful as a guide. There is a lot of discussion about whether the different levels actually relate to each other. As you can see, under the NQF, HNDs and HNCs are on the same level – how can that be when a HND takes longer? There is no simple answer – the best thing to do is to use these frameworks only as a very rough guide to how the qualifications relate to each other.

Warning #2: All of this information is correct at the time of going to press, but the various government offices that control these frameworks can't seem to stop tinkering with them, so don't be surprised if they look slightly different in the coming months. An example of this is that OCR Nationals are currently changing to become Cambridge Nationals. The important thing to remember is that whether you're choosing vocational or academic qualifications there are routes to get more qualified that are equal to the 'other side'. This is especially useful to know if you're interested in converting – switching your vocational qualifications into a degree, etc.

ACTION

Take a look at the table above and pick out some of the qualifications that you've heard of. Take a look along the same level and get familiar with the other types of qualification that you could pursue.

WHAT IS A VOCATIONAL QUALIFICATION?

Now we've seen that there are different levels for qualifications, it's important to get an idea of exactly what a vocational qualification is. The simplest explanation is that a vocational qualification is a type of training experience that helps you to get better at a specific job. Rather than an academic qualification that attempts to develop more general skills and understanding – perhaps from a wider perspective – a vocational qualification is tied specifically to a job.

As an example, if you studied engineering as an academic subject you might learn more about the background to the subject, the historical perspective, the mathematics behind the role and the various applications of the subject. It would probably involve a lot of books, learning theories and proving to an examiner that you knew and could apply that theory. If you studied engineering as a vocational qualification you would learn how to be an engineer. Your hands would get dirty doing the job and you'd end up with a very clear idea of what the job actually meant.

One of the unique things about vocational qualifications in the Qualifications and Credit Framework is that they are made up of units. You take different units related to the qualification and you get credits for that work based on how long it takes to complete. One credit is equal to about ten hours' work. The different levels of qualification under the

QCF will all need different levels of credits to complete. One of the great things about the unit system is that you can take your time to complete a qualification and build on it once you've achieved it. There are three levels of qualification which all take a different amount of time to achieve:

- Awards (1 to 12 credits – approximately 10 to 120 hours' work)
- Certificates (13 to 36 credits – approximately 130 to 360 hours' work)
- Diplomas (37 credits or more – from 370 hours' work onwards).

The unit and credit system also means that the qualification is portable. So you might choose to do some units at a further education (FE) college and some with an employer. You don't even have to complete all the units with the same college. You might move around the country but you can still find a way of getting back to your study and completing your qualification. You also have some choice about which units you take, so not every course will be the same for every student.

Choosing your vocational qualification shouldn't be as tricky as it is, and it's important that you look at the exact name of the qualification you've been offered. They might sound the same but there's a lot of difference between a BTEC certificate and a BTEC diploma – possibly hundreds of hours of difference! When selecting your qualification, make sure you check the frameworks and ask if you have any questions. It's far better to ask plenty of questions at the beginning than make a mistake based on a misconception.

TIP ✓

A word on FE colleges

You can find further education (FE) colleges around the country and they are well worth considering if you are looking for an alternative to university. Even if you are looking at doing a higher education course you could still see if it's offered by your local college – approximately 10 per cent of higher education courses are delivered by FE colleges.

The statistical picture of FE colleges suggests that their students are local and more likely to be studying part-time. Whereas university has an image of students all living, working and having fun together, the stereotypical picture of college students is that they might already be in work and are simply using the college to improve their skills. They have fun too though!

There are over 220 FE colleges in the UK and they cover a wide range of institutions from sixth form colleges to specialist centres such as art and design colleges and agriculture colleges. The range of qualifications and opportunities they present is mindblowing. Over the rest of this chapter we will give you an overview of the sort of courses you're likely to find there, but the easiest way is to investigate your local colleges yourself.

HOW MUCH DO VOCATIONAL QUALIFICATIONS COST?

One of the most interesting things about vocational qualifications is that they are largely free to people depending on age, employment status and whether or not you've tried to get qualifications before. For courses starting in 2011/12, you'll probably get your vocational qualification (level 2 or 3) paid for if you don't already have GCSEs, A levels or equivalent. In 2012/13 the same applies, but for level 2 qualifications you'll need to be under 24 and for level 3 you'll need to be under 25.

Kick-start

your active career with Apprenticeships!

Apprenticeships are a great way to kick-start your career in the sector. These work-based learning schemes allow you to gain nationally recognised qualifications while earning money!

Apprenticeships usually take between 12 and 24 months to complete. Anyone aged over 16 and not in full-time education can apply.

There's a range of intermediate level and advanced level Apprenticeships available in the sector, covering sport, fitness, playwork, caravans, the outdoors, and hair and beauty.

Visit **www.skillsactive.com/apprentice-guide** to view a step by step guide to becoming an apprentice in the sport and active leisure sector.

Fast facts

- Over 25% of young people say they'd like to work in the sport and active leisure sector
- There's been a 600% increase in sport and active leisure apprentices since 2005, with 9,342 people completing Apprenticeships in 2011
- The sector has experienced an average annual growth rate of 3.9% in recent years
- An estimated 470,000 people work in the sector, representing 1.5% of UK employment
- Despite the recession, the sector is still predicted to grow at a faster rate than the UK economy as a whole.

SkillsActive

More people.
Better skilled.
Better qualified.

Visit **www.skillsactivecareers.com** to learn about the range of career pathways available

The other option for getting courses for free is if you are on Jobseeker's Allowance or Employment and Support Allowance. There are a lot of different circumstances, so the simplest thing to do is check with your college about what you'll need to pay with regard to the course you are looking at. The big thing to remember is that if you go on and get a vocational qualification such as a level 3 BTEC then you'll boost your lifetime earnings by up to £92,000 – not a bad return on investment.

REAL LIFE

I've loved the NVQs that I've done because they give me something I can show for years in work. It also means that I can prove to my employer that I'm getting better at my job, which is useful for me as well because it means I can ask for a pay rise!

Steve

THE DIFFERENT VOCATIONAL QUALIFICATIONS

One of the differences that you'll find with vocational qualifications is that you can study several different 'brands' of qualification. Often the course that it refers to is very similar but it's accredited by a different organisation. This can still be confusing though, and it means that you'll need to know something about how they differ from each other. However, it's also a positive thing because it means that regardless of how you like to learn and what topic it is that you want to study, you're almost guaranteed to find a qualification to suit you.

One of the best places to start your search is at the official search page http://register.ofqual.gov.uk/, which is where all the officially recognised qualifications are listed. Here you can search by qualification level, organisation, qualification type and start date. When choosing which vocational qualification is right for you, it's important to look at where you can study for the particular qualification and what it comprises of. This next section should give you a brief overview of some of the most common vocational qualifications and what they are.

National Vocational Qualifications (NVQs) (also known as Scottish Vocational Qualifications, SVQs)

Based on the National Occupations Standards, NVQs work to recognise the various skills people need to do a particular job. They also exist as a framework for people who work within a particular field to show what it is that they can do to progress beyond the level they are currently at. The NVQ can be taken either as part of work or as part of an apprenticeship. The key thing about NVQs is that they involve an assessor measuring how you are doing at different elements of your job and accrediting them.

You can take an NVQ up to level 5, which is the top qualification and is roughly equivalent to a postgraduate qualification in the Framework for Higher Education Qualifications. You can get an NVQ in over 1300 different subjects, making them one of the widest ranging qualifications around. Some of the main subject areas in which you can find NVQs include:

○ business
○ sales and marketing
○ health and social care

○ food, drink and leisure
○ construction and property
○ manufacturing and engineering.

One of the key elements of the NVQ system is that you are assessed in practical ways. That means you're less likely to be sitting down and writing an exam essay, and more likely to be showing an examiner exactly how you would do a particular part of your job.

City & Guilds

City & Guilds is another very well-known name in vocational qualifications. The name City & Guilds revolves around the name of the awarding body. City & Guilds have been going for well over 100 years and were set up to formalise the training for some of the apprentices who worked in London. Since then they have continued to grow offering training across the world in over 500 different areas. City & Guilds work with industry and employers to develop their qualifications and you can be sure that with a City & Guilds you'll develop the skills you need to succeed in your career.

City & Guilds offers a series of NVQ, SVQ and VRQ schemes and its qualifications can be studied up to Level 8. Every year nearly 2 million people receive a City & Guilds' qualification, in sectors that include hairdressing to hospitality; construction to care; and finance to floristry. City & Guilds wants to inspire people to discover their potential, aim high and most importantly, believe in what they can achieve.

BTECs

BTECs are a type of vocational qualification designed and delivered by a company called Edexcel. They are designed to work as an alternative to GCSEs and A levels, but still allow for progression to higher forms

CASE STUDY

Marc Roberts

Marc is currently undertaking the Level 3 Diploma in Work Based Animal Care (Zoo's/Wildlife Route) at Noah's Ark Zoo Farm, where he has been working for 18 months

As an Apprentice Keeper, Marc shadows the keepers on their day-to-day jobs, acquiring the skills he needs to work with animals in the long term. Marc's team, which includes senior zoo keepers and fellow apprentices, helps with the daily care of many zoo and exotic species including rhino, giraffes, big cats, primates and reptiles. After a year he was trained to work with every animal in the collection and able to cover keepers when they were away from their sections.

Marc's daily routine with the big zoo animal section includes checking the rhino in the morning, and giraffe feeding and cleaning. Along with exotics, similar morning feed preparation and cleaning is carried out for red deer, sheep, llamas, goats, cows, camels and reindeer. Afternoon tasks usually focus on on-going jobs, maintenance of enclosures and enrichment of animals, once feeding and cleaning duties in the morning are complete. The final tasks for the day include putting animals away for the night and securing the zoo before closure. Marc also comes into contact with zoo visitors

when doing animal shows and talks; he is trained to present the Big Cat Feeding Talk - one of the main events of the day.

When trying to get a job in the animal industry, work experience is key; Marc started volunteering at Noah's Ark just after turning 17. He began college in September that same year, studying the Animal Management National Diploma. The diploma lasted two years and Marc continued to volunteer at Noah's Ark for one day a week. In addition, during the summer holidays between his first and second year he undertook a five-week work experience trip to South Africa on a game reserve to further boost his knowledge.

Towards the end of college Marc was offered the apprenticeship at Noah's Ark, which has enabled substantial hands-on experience. Now Marc is coming to the end of his apprenticeship and has been offered a job at the zoo to continue working as a keeper.

For more information visit City & Guilds
www.cityandguilds.com

of learning if you wish. The difference between BTECs and NVQs is that while NVQs are based in the workplace and seek to formalise what you have learned and how you can progress when in a job, a BTEC is a qualification that teaches you about a particular job. You should expect more of a balance between classroom and practical work with a BTEC.

BTECs are very well respected by employers around the world, and as they have been in use for more than 25 years there is a good chance that any company you apply to will have at least heard of your qualification. One of the reasons that BTECs are well respected is because they are designed with the help of employers, who express what skills they would like new workers to have. As with most vocational qualifications you can study for a BTEC at several different levels:

- **Entry** – for learners to develop confidence and initial skills.
- **Introductory (level 1)** – a basic introduction to an industry sector.
- **Nationals (level 3)** – specialist qualifications for students who know what they want to do.
- **Higher Nationals (level 5)** – higher education qualifications recognised by universities.
- **Development and Professional Development qualifications (levels 4–8)** – short courses for professional development.

Foundation degrees

If you're looking for a halfway point between a standard university degree and a vocational qualification, then a foundation degree might be just what you need. A foundation degree is done at university and lasts for two years (or three to four years part-time). It works in much the same way as an apprenticeship does in that it balances theory and practical study to give you a much more rounded education. You can choose to study a foundation degree in hundreds of different subjects.

The foundation degree is designed so that it can be done while you are working and obviously it will benefit you most if you are working in an area connected to the subject you are studying, but it's not essential. You will have at least some exposure to related work experience if you are doing a foundation degree. In this sense it can be seen as an excellent way to get contacts in an area.

For foundation degrees you are assessed through a mixture of work-based assessments, project work and exams. This differs depending on the individual course so check with your university. When you complete a foundation degree you can either 'top up' the learning into a full degree, with another year of studying, or look for work opportunities in your chosen field.

Functional skills

Functional Skills courses are vocational qualifications in the wider sense that they attempt to equip you with some of the abilities you need to thrive in the workplace. Key Skills courses are offered at a number of FE colleges and training providers. They are designed to equip learners with knowledge about some of the essential elements of work and the working world. The three areas you can study Functional Skills in are:

- Mathematics
- English
- Information and Communication Technology.

If you're concerned that you don't have the evidence of a particular element, or you feel that you're weaker in one area, then a Functional Skills course can be a good way of improving or showing an employer that you are qualified. Functional Skills are accessible to anyone regardless of age or position. If you are doing an apprenticeship and some other vocational qualifications then you will have to do Functional Skills courses alongside them.

Cambridge Nationals (also known as OCR Nationals)

As with other vocational qualifications such as City & Guilds and BTECs, the real difference with Cambridge Nationals is that they are awarded by a particular examining body. The qualifications that they have devised are aimed at equipping students with the skills they will need to get into work. As well as equipping them with industry skills they develop work-related skills such as team-working, communication and problem solving. These qualifications are mainly aimed at those aged 14–19 in full- or part-time study.

Higher National Certificates (HNCs) and Higher National Diplomas (HNDs)

HNCs and HNDs are aimed at those students who want to progress to higher education but who want to study something with a far greater vocational content.

HNCs take one year to complete full-time, two years part-time and HNDs take two years full-time and usually three to four years part-time. If you knew that you really wanted to work in any of the following areas then the HNC/HND route allows you to study the particular skills you will need to work in that area:

- O Agriculture
- O Computing and IT
- O Engineering
- O Health and social care
- O Sport and exercise sciences
- O Performing arts
- O Retail and distribution
- O Hospitality management.

This is by no means an exhaustive list and there's a good chance that whatever career you're settled on you will be able to find an HND/HNC to help you achieve it. They are provided by over 400 different universities and FE colleges, and as you would expect with vocational courses they largely assess through practical examination of skills, rather than straightforward exams. In much the same way as a foundation degree a HNC/HND can be converted to a full degree with extra study.

THE CHOICE IS YOURS

The range of vocational qualifications is expanding all the time and we've only been able to give an overview of the different options open to you. As suggested, the best thing to do when you are offered a qualification is first to assess whether it is the right level for you – so take a look at what it is equivalent to in the different frameworks and ask if you would be able to study comfortably at that level. Once you've established that, you can take a closer look at how the course is delivered and what it comprises of. Again, your FE college, university or training provider should be able to give you a much better indication of the different merits of a type of course. As ever, research before you engage and get a range of opinions on how useful a particular course could be.

Find out where your local FE college is and when they are holding their next open day. They host these throughout the year and they're the perfect opportunity to get a taste of what vocational qualifications can do for you.

CASE STUDY

Peter Kernan

After training for a Level 3 Diploma in Wood Occupations (Site). Peter has carved out a successful career working on some of Britain's best-loved landmarks

Peter Kernan shows exactly what can be achieved with drive, enthusiasm and a passion for your trade. Peter first became interested in the building sector when he accepted a job working for a building company during his summer holidays.

As the summer progressed, it became apparent to his employer that Peter had an exceptional talent for carpentry and he was soon offered the chance to enrol on a City & Guilds Level 3 Diploma in Wood Occupations (Site). Peter excelled in his learning and by the time he had completed his course in 2010, he had developed his skills to a very high standard.

Aside from working towards completing his course, he also challenged himself on the competition circuit, participating in the National Skillbuild competition in Wales. The competition required him to showcase the range of skills he had developed whilst taking his course.

As a result of participating in the competition, Peter was selected to represent his country at WorldSkills in London in 2011. However, just after he was selected to be part of the UK team, Peter was offered the chance of a lifetime - he was accepted by the Prince's Foundation to work alongside Master Craftsmen on historic buildings including Windsor Castle and York Minster. It was an opportunity that was too good to be missed and Peter went on to work with Master Carpenters at Windsor Castle and complete his Level 3 NVQ heritage work.

Peter has continued to be an inspiration to his friends, family and colleagues; last year, he won a City & Guilds Medal for Excellence for his achievements and went on to be named Outstanding Achiever of the Year at City & Guilds' annual Lion Awards.

Peter says: 'Winning an award like that really makes you believe you have the ability to get the best jobs out there. At the moment, I'm happy at Windsor Castle, but I would like to own my own business one day. It's inspiring restoring something that's been there for hundreds of years and might be there for hundreds more."

For more information visit City & Guilds
www.cityandguilds.com

BREAK THE MOULD

PETER JONES
ENTERPRISE
ACADEMY

The Peter Jones Enterprise Academy courses provide young people who have entrepreneurial drive and ambition with the wealth of knowledge, skills and experience needed to start their own business.

If you're an Entrepreneur this is the time!'

Peter Jones CBE,
Founder of the Peter Jones
Enterprise Academy

Our three courses are unique.

BTEC Level 3 in Enterprise and Entrepreneurship

In just one year students acquire the skills, experience and confidence to develop and run a business. Over 50% of the curriculum is taught by real business people — truly bringing the boardroom to the classroom!

Advanced Apprenticeship in Enterprise

Ever thought I could do that better? This first ever non-occupational apprenticeship will enable you to grow the productivity, profitability and competitiveness of the company you work for. Working over 18 months in a role such as Business Development Executive or Enterprise Consultant you will develop skills in problem solving, innovative practises and resourcefulness through a mix of on—and off—the job learning.

Higher Apprenticeship in Innovation and Growth (starting in March 2013)

Our fastest route to becoming a leader in business. If you are interested in the idea of working for an organisation which is looking to grow and to do things differently, and you'd like the opportunity to help them do just that, then this could be just what you are looking for. Over 18 months you will acquire a 'toolkit' of business knowledge, but the emphasis throughout will be on applying innovative approaches and carrying out innovative projects.

The Academy courses are taught in 36 different locations across England.* For a full list visit: **www.pjea.org/colleges**

Visit **www.pjea.org** to register your interest in the Peter Jones Enterprise Academy.

PETER JONES
FOUNDATION

*not all of our providers offer all three qualifications.

CHAPTER SEVEN

HOW TO GET A JOB

This chapter in brief

- One in five people under 25 are in employment.

- But two in five under 25s are unemployed.

- When competition is tough you have to be extra careful about how you apply for jobs.

- Speculative applications can land you a job when none supposedly exist.

- Interviews can be fun!

- Starting your own business after you leave school is a fantastic idea.

For many school leavers when they slam the school door shut behind them, they never want to do any kind of education again. Around 20 per cent of under 25s are in employment – so looking to move straight into a job is a popular option for those leaving education. It's a completely understandable position to take. After all, you've spent nearly two decades being told what to learn, what to read, what to wear – it's about time you had some freedom. However, it's important not to close off any options – education is a lifelong process. If you're one of those who just wants to get a job when they leave school, this chapter is for you.

But before you head to the job centre it's worth understanding the current employment situation. In a word, it's not great. It may not have escaped your attention, but the UK, Europe and the world are currently experiencing some of the toughest markets ever. There is a global recession (a recession is simply a long period when the economy is on the decline) and that means that companies are less likely to invest and grow their businesses, which also means that they don't create new jobs. Some of the recent statistics in the UK make for worrying reading – it's sobering to think that two in five under 25s are unemployed. For the first time in decades the number of under 25s out of work topped 1 million. That's scary stuff.

There's really no need to panic though. The jobs are out there if you can find them and with research and planning that's precisely what you can do. With a careful and methodical application plan you can massively increase your chances of getting any job you apply for. In short, you have to do quite a lot of work simply to get into work. There's no point complaining about it though – it's a tough situation but it's the same for everyone. Follow our instructions and you'll stand a good chance of being the one in five who are employed, rather than the two in five who are unemployed.

PLAN YOUR SEARCH

Fortunately, as you closely read and followed Chapters 1 and 2 you'll have a very clear idea of what career it is that you want to work in. Wait! You mean you haven't already done your career planning research?

ACTION

If you haven't worked through the first two chapters, turn to the front, find a pen and get working. Throwing yourself into work without any idea of what you want to do is a recipe for job dissatisfaction and a less-than-perfect working life. Don't set off in the wrong direction just because you can't spare the time to do some planning.

In many ways it's more important that you have an idea about where you want to end up if you're not taking the option of getting extra training when you leave school. You might not find the perfect job straight away, but you can at least target roles that get your foot in the door of companies where your dream occupation actually goes on. For example, if you've always wanted to work as a journalist, it's far better to look for temporary, starter or unrelated roles in publishing companies who employ journalists. Otherwise you'll simply be moving further and further away from your dream.

REAL LIFE

I started my working life as a delivery man for a huge broadcaster. It always made me laugh that every job they advertised had thousands of applicants, but only four people went for the mail man role. It was hard work, but I got to know the organisation

> inside out and it made it so much easier to know where the opportunities were going to come up, and my next role wasn't even advertised. I just said I knew how to do it and they created the role for me.
>
> *Mark*

The other reason that it's important to do some solid career research is that it allows you to know what your skills are and also to build up contacts in an industry. Knowing what you are good at makes it a lot easier when it comes to writing a CV, or talking to an interview panel about why they should employ you. Plus asking someone for work experience or to be a work shadow is always going to be easier than asking them outright for a job. And once you've impressed on a short placement, or made a good contact with the boss of a company, it's amazing how much more likely you are to hear about opportunities before they become public knowledge.

So, assuming you've done your research (see the Action box above if not!), you can afford yourself a moment of congratulatory back-slapping. You know where you want to end up, you know what sort of skills you've got that make you right for that sort of role. You've investigated the job and built up some contacts who you can speak to about the different job opportunities that come up. Before you even fill in the first application form you've already given yourself a better chance than 90 per cent of the rest of the candidates. Now it's time to really make that advantage show.

TIP ✓

The experience trap

One of the most common complaints from job-hunters is that companies are looking for people with experience to do the job. Many young people complain that this is especially unfair because they haven't yet had the opportunity to build up the experience. While this is completely understandable, it's also a trap. You are allowing yourself to believe that you are locked out of the job market, as if it's some kind of vendetta against everyone who is under the age of 30. Do not give in to the temptation to complain.

Think of it from the company's viewpoint. Yes, it would be easier to think of them as evil fat cats who are trying to destroy the youth of today, but that's not the case. In point of fact, they would love it if someone came to them who could do the job who was younger, because younger equals cheaper. As people get older they typically get better at their jobs and get pay rises (or they don't get better and they lose their job). Better people means that they get paid more. Younger people with lower living costs are a dream for employers.

So how do you get experience then? First you need to identify what it is that a recruiter wants experience in. If they say that they want you to have a particular skill, such as a computer language, then you either get the skill through a course, or hold your hands up and admit that you might not be ready for this job. However, if it's evidence of a more general skill then you work through your past experiences (see Chapters 1 and 2 for background on how to do this) and see where you've got evidence of that particular skill. Then you sell it to them. Talk in terms of years, positions of responsibility, situations you controlled.

If you haven't got the experience then maybe you're looking at a job that you haven't properly prepared for (back to Chapters 1 and 2 again) and you're going to need either to go and get qualifications, or to look for opportunities through volunteering, contacts or travelling where you can develop that sort of experience. Nothing is impossible to someone who is willing to think flexibly. Every time you come up against a barrier, learn to enjoy the process of smashing it down.

Whatever you do – don't allow yourself to fall into the experience trap.

WHERE TO FIND THE VACANCIES

Because there are so many different places to look for work, one of the most complex tasks in finding the right position for you can be working out where you should start looking. Return to the research you did on case studies and job profiles. These will have suggested some of the different places that vacancies in your chosen profession will be advertised and discussed. Make these your first port of call when signing up for email alerts or looking at which papers or magazines to buy (or borrow from the local library).

At the beginning of the job-hunting process you want to cast your net as wide as possible. Sign up for as many websites and agencies as you like, tell as many people as possible what you're looking for, start to politely approach your network of contacts and tell them what you're after. Don't forget to filter your results though, and refine the search on those sources that are producing the best information. It's much better to have to read through a lot of not-quite-perfect opportunities than to get frustrated that you're not getting a single result.

Here are some of the sources you should approach to generate the different vacancies:

1. Jobcentre Plus

The government has several different ways of helping you in your search for gainful employment and the key to accessing them is through your Jobcentre Plus. You might have the idea that Jobcentre Plus is mainly for older people who have been made redundant, but its services are designed to help school leavers just as much as more mature workers.

To access help through Jobcentre Plus you would need to be registered to receive Jobseeker's Allowance (known as JSA, which works out as £53.45 per week for young people who are looking for work). To register for JSA, call the hotline on 0800 0556688. Once you're registered you will be assigned an appointment with an advisor through your nearest Jobcentre Plus. However, don't forget that anyone can access their database of jobs (which happens to be the largest in the UK) and apply for them online by visiting www.direct.gov.uk/whatsnext.

2. Recruitment agencies

There are thousands of recruitment agencies across the UK who can help find you work. Always remember that agencies get paid by taking a percentage of your wage, so it's in their interest to get you into work. In some cases though, this means they're not always interested in finding the right job for you. To find the best agency for you, have a look at the Recruitment and Employment Confederation website (www. rec.uk.com) and use their consultancy finder, which should give you a number of agencies who specialise in the type of work you'd like to find.

Registering involves going in to see a recruitment consultant and telling them what work you're looking for. Research the sort of vacancies that the agency has before you see them to save wasting anyone's time – and in many cases you might be able to register online. Don't try applying to 30 agencies all at once as you'll probably end up with a quantity of offers, rather than the quality ones. Select two or three and add more if none of these produce the right sort of vacancies. Once you are registered keep in regular, polite contact with your consultant so you become one of the first people they think of when a good job comes up.

3. Papers and websites

There are hundreds of websites and publications that carry job adverts, so many that it makes creating a list of them almost impossible. Through your careers research you should have identified some of the main ones for careers in your chosen profession. Although the national papers often carry positions that are for employees with more experience, you can still find entry level positions advertised. Papers advertise jobs for different industries on specific days – to get an idea of when your favoured industry is featured have a look at http://www.open.ac.uk/careers/advertised-jobs.php. Your local paper will also be a great starting point for jobs and it's highly likely that the paper will have at least some of the jobs that it features on its website. Other websites such as www.fish4jobs.co.uk and www.totaljobs .com carry thousands of jobs and allow you to search by area as well as position.

4. Social networks

Many employers have started using sites such as Facebook and LinkedIn as part of their recruitment process and claim that jobseekers with strong online profiles who network well are more likely to be hired. To take advantage of this, make sure you have signed up to relevant social networks and that your profile would impress business contacts or prospective employers. Use your social network profile to track vacancies and recruitment consultancies and network strategically to connect with people who can help with your job search.

5. By investigating companies' opportunities directly

Many companies have recruitment schemes where they look for the brightest school leavers to train up on their own internal training schemes. This wouldn't necessarily result in a qualification, but you would get a full wage and you would also be fast-tracked for promotion within the company and supported through all your training. If you're interested in working for a particular company, then have a look at their website and see if they run a school-leaver scheme, or send a polite email to their HR department asking what options they have.

TIP ✓

Speculative applications

This statistic might seem particularly unfair to anyone who has spent hours scanning the Wanted ads and waiting in queues at the job centre, but there are plenty of jobs out there that will never be advertised. You might find references to this as the 'hidden job market' and see estimates of anywhere from 30 per cent to 80 per cent of jobs not being advertised. There is no definitive study of how big the hidden job market is, but it does offer a valid point about job-hunting, namely that you have to create your own opportunities.

There is an art to creating your own opportunities and it's advisable to understand that you're probably not going to get it right first time. Your sales pitch will take a few goes until it's perfect, but when you've got it cracked you'll find that you have learned a skill that will see you getting employed many times over the course of your career. A speculative application works because it proves that you have identified a need that a company has and that you are the person to solve that.

Clearly you're going to have to be really good at business to examine the structure of, say, a massive supermarket's logistics operation and go in and be able to solve it. However, staying with the example of a supermarket, you might be able to see that a supermarket doesn't bring much traffic in off the road and you might be able to approach the manager, explain the situation and offer a solution – say you standing there with a 'Supermarket Open' sign on the main road. These are at two ends of a scale but they rely on precisely the same process:

1   Identify a problem that is costing the business money or something that they could improve on.
2   Pinpoint how you would solve that problem in a cost-effective way.
3   Take the problem and the solution to someone high up.

There really is nothing more to it than that. In each situation point 3 will differ. Sometimes you might be writing to a company, or you could go in person to explain the problem and solution. In most cases, if nothing else, you will have shown someone high up that you are capable of spotting problems and working out solutions, which is precisely the sort of thinking process that they will look for in employees.

The way that you approach them will show that you can sell yourself and communicate in an excellent and convincing manner. Don't forget that if you're pointing out something they could do better then you will need to be diplomatic – don't just say they're not very good! The whole thing is like a job interview that you have created for yourself.

As for whether or not it works, well that depends on whether or not the person you're talking to a) agrees that it is a problem and b) agrees that your solution is the easiest and most cost effective. Sometimes you might find that they take your solution and steal it – that's all part of the risk, but provided it hasn't cost you anything then you've not lost too much.

The brilliant thing is that when you hone your ability to spot these situations (and it's really something that everyone can do) you very quickly come to realise that the world is full of these situations. You have developed the entrepreneur's mindset and that is something that will pay off for the rest of your life.

HOW TO APPLY

CVs

Although it's becoming more common for job applications to be processed online, by far the most popular form of application remains the dreaded curriculum vitae (CV) and covering letter. Although it's easy to be tricked into writing more informally in an email, don't think that your covering email should be any less formal than a letter. This is your first chance to sell yourself to an employer, so make the most of it.

Over two-thirds of companies still use CVs and interviews to recruit, so you'd better accept that you need to sort yours out. Your CV is the first impression an employer will get of you and it's what they will use to choose whether to invite you for an interview. Therefore, it's important to spend time getting it right. Your chance of being selected for an interview can depend on how well you sell yourself at this point, so your CV should be full of all the best examples of why you are right for the particular job you are going for.

There are some basic rules you need to follow for CVs. First of all, keep your CV to a maximum of two sides of A4 paper. Employers receive a lot of CVs and it's unlikely that they will read each one from start to finish. Most will make a judgement about a CV after a few seconds, so keep it as short and to the point as possible. Read the job description over and over again until you have a very clear idea of what skills the employer wants to see evidenced on your CV – then make sure that you deliver that experience. If you think you fall short then do your best to explain how your experiences have trained you for this post perfectly. Do not lie!

It's also important to make sure that your CV is up to date and that it looks good. Make sure that at least two other people check for spelling mistakes, poor grammar and any missing information that could see your CV winging its way to the nearest bin.

Every CV should contain contact details, personal information, academic and professional history, your skills relevant to the job, interests and references. Although these examples (http://www.kent.ac.uk/careers/cv/cvexamples.htm) are for graduates who might have more work experience than you, they should give you a good guide as to the format you're aiming for and some thoughts on how to start putting your experiences together.

Your references should come from people who know you well and can tell an employer about what you have done in the past. They are usually your last two employers, but if you haven't worked before you can use a teacher or a tutor from school or college. It's polite and advisable to ask your referees for their permission before putting their names down.

ACTION ⚡

Check your current CV, read through it as if you were receiving it. What are the key messages that jump out at you – could you find three reasons that it sells you as a candidate?

Covering letters

Your covering letter (or covering email if the employer has asked you to email your CV) is the first chance you have to sell yourself to an employer. Use it to draw the employer's attention to the most important information in your CV, such as your skills and experience. This should be the sections of your experience and qualifications that directly match with the employer's job description.

A cover letter allows you to introduce yourself to your prospective employer, explain your background and level of expertise, and highlight your strengths and enthusiasm. Make sure your letter says more than simply that your CV is enclosed. Use it to reconfirm and expand on your areas of expertise.

Be careful that you don't come across as arrogant as this will put employers off. Similarly, don't go for jokes as this simply isn't appropriate. Being creative might work if you are going for a job in advertising or marketing but could leave other employers slightly bemused. The best idea is to communicate your enthusiasm for the job, ask yourself why you really want this job and use that as the basis for your covering letter.

TIP ✓

CV and covering letter – dos and don'ts

○ **Do** pick a font that is clear and easy to read, making sure each section is clearly headed and well-formatted.

○ **Do** remember, a CV is an opportunity to sell yourself. Take the time to go through the job description and try to demonstrate how your skills and experience match up. You want to convince the employer that you are the perfect recruit for their company.

○ **Do** get the length right. Employers often have to plough through hundreds of CVs for each vacancy. Keep it no longer than two pages. Stick to the point and avoid waffle.

○ **Do** put your qualifications in reverse order starting with the most recent.

○ **Don't** forget to place your correct contact details in a prominent place. You wouldn't want to miss out on an opportunity because an employer wasn't able to get in touch.

○ **Don't** lie. If you exaggerate information about your level of experience or the skills that you have and your employer finds out, you could face the sack.

○ **Don't** list lots of information about your hobbies unless they're relevant to the job or show a quality such as teamworking.

INTERVIEWS

If you're invited to attend an interview for a job then you've already managed to pass the first stage and impressed your prospective employers with your CV. The next step is to impress them in person.

Before the interview – preparation

When you are invited to an interview the first thing you should do is spend some time researching your potential employer. This will give you the confidence to answer any questions on what the company does and the background knowledge to ask the employer any questions.

Read up about your potential future employer on the company website or contact the company directly to ask for an information pack. Find out the following things about the employer:

O   What they do, make or sell
O   Who their target customers, clients or audience are
O   How the company is structured
O   What the job is likely to involve
O   What skills you have that are matched to the job.

It's important to make practical plans as well. Consider travelling to the company the day before the interview to check how long the journey will take. If necessary, ask the employer for directions, bus routes or details of where you can park your car. You should plan another way of getting there in case something unexpected happens (such as an accident blocking the road, or your train being cancelled). If you have a disability, let the employer know so they can make any special arrangements.

REAL LIFE

This is shameful. Let's just say that staying out until you can see the sun coming up means you're not going to be very good at an interview the next day. During the meeting the interviewer handed me a pen so I could make a note. I tried for ages pushing the end to get the pen bit to poke out. In the end the interviewer took the pen off me and twisted it. The pen bit poked out. How was I supposed to know it was a twist?

Absolutely, definitely someone who is not the author
of this book

Deciding what to wear for the interview will depend on what sort of work you will be doing. Decide what to wear and get your clothes ready the day before. You don't have to buy a new outfit. Aim for a neat, clean and tidy appearance – if you look good it will help you feel good. It's always easier to wear a suit or smart skirt and smart shoes and take off your tie or your jacket if you look too formal, rather than try to look smarter in jeans and T-shirt.

You will need to get any relevant paperwork ready. On the day you'll need to take a copy of your CV or application form to refer to. You could prepare notes or cue cards to help if you might need a prompt during the interview. Also, don't forget to take any items the employer has asked from you such as references, certificates or your driving licence. It's also helpful to re-read the job advert to refresh your memory and to make sure you haven't missed anything.

On the day – we know this sounds weird but enjoy it!

Do you want to know a secret about nerves? They are simply your body's way of making sure you take something seriously. If you prepare really well for an interview you will not be nervous, in fact you can start to turn it around and look forward to it. How is that possible? Because you'll have so many great things to tell the interviewers about. So many reasons why you're the perfect person for the job that you can be confident and enjoy it!

You can help yourself out by giving yourself plenty of time to get ready and make sure you've got all the relevant paperwork with you. If you are delayed, contact the employer as soon as possible to explain, apologise and arrange another appointment. You should aim to arrive at least 20 minutes before the interview time. When you arrive give your name to the receptionist or whoever is there to greet you.

In the interview all you have to do is let your research do its work. Tell them why you are excited about this job and why you are perfect for it; back it up with evidence and you will be in with a very strong chance. When answering questions, stay positive and polite.

If you have a fast heartbeat or sweaty hands, remember these are your body's natural way of meeting a challenge, and in small doses this burst of adrenaline can help you. If you're nervous your voice may give you away so practise deep, slow breathing before you get to the interview. This will slow down your heart rate and help you avoid taking quick shallow breaths.

Don't forget that an interview is a two-way process, so take an interest in what your interviewer says about the company. Ask any questions about the company or what your job would entail.

STARTING YOUR OWN COMPANY – AN IMPOSSIBLE DREAM?

Who on earth leaves school and starts their own business? It's preposterous! It just doesn't happen! Who would lend you the money?

What business would you start up? Who would take you seriously? How would you know what to do? Ridiculous! If that's the sort of thing going through your head then a) calm down and b) you'd be surprised. The Prince's Trust each year helps over 50,000 13–30 year olds and many of them set up their own businesses. So they go from being bossed around at school by teachers every day to being their own boss in one move. Sound attractive? Then let's deal with some of those questions.

What business would you start up?

Now, that's an intriguing question. Earlier in this chapter we looked at speculative applications and identifying problems. The point was that if you can spot a problem or something that's missing from a business and work out how to correct it then you have started to condition your entrepreneur muscle. Although biologists probably wouldn't agree, this business muscle works exactly the same as any other muscle. The more you flex it and use it to spot opportunities and work out how you would service that opportunity, the better it gets. Before long you'll be generating ten ideas a week. Then it'll be ten a day. Before long you'll find an idea that really excites you.

One of the biggest lies about starting a business is that you need to come up with an original idea or product. It's not true. It certainly helps if your business is in a relatively new (and developing) area, or if it's built on the back of exciting new technology, but frankly the business that launches into a completely new area is often the only one there because it's not something that customers want. It's much better to work out how to properly run a company and launch a business into an existing market than it is to spend 30 years waiting for inspiration to strike.

Adrian Jarrett

The Peter Jones Academy
BTEC Level 3 Enterprise and Entrepreneurship

From an early age I knew I wanted to run my own business. Being an actor, I'd always wanted to focus on a creative career where I could earn a living, as well as gain total job satisfaction liaising with people offering a multitude of talents.

When considering my options for further education, I came across the BTEC Level 3 Diploma in Enterprise and Entrepreneurship, awarded by The Peter Jones Enterprise Academy at Solihull College. After applying for the course I was invited to the College for an induction and I fell in love with the wonderful facilities on offer. The relaxed atmosphere was extremely welcoming and the College had a great reputation for its strong student support.

For me, the best part of the course is that it makes you think outside the box. It not only teaches you about setting up a business, it also allows you to adopt the mindset of an entrepreneur. It provides you with in-depth knowledge about fundamental business principles whilst focusing on your individual business goals. The jump from being in a nurtured school environment, to one which is more independent, was a challenge, but I have overcome this by setting myself small achievable goals and pushing myself to excel.

Aside from specific business related units, we also get involved with fun activities during the course; collectively our group raised over £3,500 for national charity, Teenage Cancer Trust. To raise funds, I took part in the Birmingham Half Marathon 2011. Crossing the finish line was one of my proudest moments to date, I still wear my wrist band everyday – it was such a rewarding experience.

I have been lucky to have several strong influences in my life, my elder brother and teachers to name a few, but since studying at The Peter Jones Enterprise Academy, I can add my peers to these influences too. Whilst we all have different career goals, we all want the same from the course – to be successful. It's great to be able to learn from each other's experiences. The tutors have also been instrumental in helping me to succeed so far, their knowledge, guidance and support has been fantastic.

For more information visit
www.peterjonesfoundation.org

This is where going back to the first two chapters can help. If you can identify the sort of career you'd like to pursue, then it might well be that you can pinpoint the right business area for you and rather than looking for work, simply set up your own business in that area.

Who would lend you the money?

There are lots of routes to secure funding, certainly more than you'd think. After all, investing in businesses is one way that people make money for themselves. So if you can convince people, whether it's a bank manager, a relative or an angel investor (like on *Dragons' Den*), that your business is going places then they would be crazy not to give you the money, providing they can make a decent rate of interest from it as well.

The following are some of the most common sources of business funding:

- Family
- Organisations
- Banks
- Business loans
- Investors
- Other grants and loans (e.g. charities, kickstarter funding).

Of course this assumes that you would need funding in the first place. In actual fact it's far easier to start a very small business with practically zero funding and see if you can make money from this light business model. This could provide enough capital for you to invest. For instance, if you wanted to make cakes, you wouldn't go straight out and buy a bakery, you could cook cakes at home and sell them to friends. If they were really popular you could look at scaling up this business.

REAL LIFE

When I left school I wish I'd known how much easier and better it is in every way to work for yourself, not someone else. Everything you need to know is in the pages of *How to Get Rich* by Felix Dennis, including why actually getting rich is probably not a very smart move.

Matt

So how do you start your own business?

It's actually far simpler than you realise. Businesses need just one thing – a product that customers will buy. So once you've worked out what your product (or service) is going to be, you take that to the customers using sales and marketing techniques. You do the job, sell the product. Finally, you finesse the business, so you work out how to get a greater profit margin on your product or service and attract more customers. It doesn't matter how complicated a business looks – whether it's offshore derivatives, nuclear power or running a hairdressers, all you need is a product or service that customers will buy. Then you need more customers.

A great way to experiment with self-employment is to try it on your own time – the bakery mentioned above is one example. But let's say that you've always wanted to be a hairdresser and you've spent years working on Saturdays in a salon. You've got a good idea of what works and what makes money and you've done your training through an apprenticeship or a course. Why not give it a go? All you'd need is a minimum of equipment and set up as a mobile hairdresser. Offer cheap haircuts to see if you enjoy it and if you can do it (it also reduces the pressure on the client). If you find that after ten or 15 cuts it's something you love, then try increasing your output.

Put a small advert in the supermarket wanted ads, or a tiny ad in the paper. Keep an eye on what you spend as these are your overheads and need careful recording. Also keep a close eye on what you earn as this is your turnover. If you minus the overheads away from the turnover you have your profit. It can be easy to look at all the cash coming in and forget that you've got to pay for petrol, or get some more equipment. An ancient law of business says that:

Turnover is for the vain, profit is for the sane.

What that means is that if you start a business and look at how fantastic your earnings are, before you minus what you have to spend you'll probably go insane! And that's it really. **Start small, investigate, expand.** If at any point you feel that it's not going well, pull the plug. Think again. Work out what it is that you don't like and try again.

People always think that having a business must be an incredible pressure, because what happens if it fails? If you start small and build up you'll know that it works before it gets big enough to be a stress. And if at some point it fails then who cares? If you've learned how to avoid making the same mistake in the future then you've simply bought yourself some valuable experience. Make things easy on yourself and you'll see that actually starting a business is by no means ridiculous for anyone, no matter how old they are.

ACTION

Forget reality, forget why you can't, turn to the Notes section and outline what sort of business you would really love to start up. What would it be called? Where would you be based? What product or service would you sell? Now – ask yourself how you could run a trial version of that exact same business.

GET ON

the Whitbread journey and join the largest and most successful hospitality group in the UK...
...and get qualified too!

WE INVEST £3 MILLION ON TRAINING EVERY YEAR

At Whitbread we are serious abo our people. We invest in training and development for all our peop at every level and you can earn qualifications whilst you are workin for us. With the growth in our busin there are loads of opportunities fo you to start your career and we pri ourselves on promoting from withi

SHOOTING STARS

Whitbread's award winning Shooting management development program are focused on supporting high pot Team Members/Managers progress their next roles and become our fut leaders. Each programme is aligned national accredited qualifications sh you choose to achieve one.

OVER 80% OF OUR MANAGEMENT ROLES ARE FILLED FROM OUR EXISTING TEAM.

There's never been a better time to work for Whitbread Hotels & Restaurants. We're the largest hospitality group in the UK, with plans to increase the number of Premier Inn rooms by nearly 50% to 65,000 and add 80-100 new restaurants.

Intermediate Apprenticeship

We offer intermediate Apprenticeships in Reception, Food & Drink Service & Food Production & Cooking. These Apprenticeships are designed to get people off to a good start in their chosen career and once achieved can open up a range of further opportunities and can lead to an Advanced Apprenticeship.

Advanced Apprenticeship in Hospitality & Supervision

Higher Apprenticeship in Hospitality Management
(coming soon)

WARNING! THESE PROGRAMMES WIL SERIOUSLY CHANG THE WAY YOU THIN

Learn more by visiting
www.thewhitbreadjourney.co.uk

 or find us on Facebook

EAT SLEEP & DRINK
WHITBREAD

CHAPTER EIGHT

THE THREE LESSONS YOU REALLY NEED TO SUCCEED IN LIFE

This chapter in brief

- Opportunities of all kinds can be created at will.

- The ability to sell is essential and it starts with the ability to sell yourself.

- Failure is not only an option, failure is brilliant! Make failure part of your future.

- The top three good career habits: handshakes, building contacts, politeness.

Schools are weird. They're adamant that you need to know quadratic equations but they don't want to teach you how to sell something. Now, there's a very good chance that you'll never need to use a quadratic equation ever again (but that's not to say that they're not hugely important, just that their inner workings won't be something you'll be called upon to use every day), but everyone will have to sell something, whether it's a product, an argument or an idea, every day for the rest of their life. So it makes sense to learn how to do it well then, right? Likewise your school probably insisted on you knowing various battle dates and styles of high jump – but they never thought to tell you that failing is fantastic or that opportunities could be created at will. Weird.

That's why in this chapter we've whittled down the various lessons that will become vital once you leave formal education into three simple tutorials. If you can master the three things you're about to learn then your life will be radically different. You will go from being someone who life happens to, to someone who is in control of their own fortunes. Remember the promise we made you at the start of this book: that you could do anything you wanted? Well, understanding and mastering these three lessons will make that come true for you. It's important stuff.

LESSON 1 – OPPORTUNITIES CAN BE CREATED AT WILL

The thought that you can create opportunities at the drop of a hat is an exciting idea, because there's nothing worse than feeling like you're trapped in a situation you can't control. Take the job world, for example – it's a desperate thing when you sit and wait for a job to come up and nothing does. It makes you feel like life is against you somehow, and that can lead to bitterness. However, creating opportunities can happen in any other aspect of life too – relationships, money, whatever you care to mention. So what's the secret? Well, like all good processes, it's achieved in three steps:

- ○ Step one: state very clearly what you want to happen.
- ○ Step two: research and plan ways to make it happen.
- ○ Step three: keep going until it happens.

If you're looking at the first step and thinking this is a con because really all we're saying is work hard, then you're partially right – working hard and trying different approaches is indeed one of the secrets to life. The name Samuel Goldwyn should ring a bell, he was one of the famous producers behind the Metro-Goldwyn-Mayer film studio. He achieved incredible things in his lifetime and when questioned about how he'd done it he noted, 'The harder I work, the luckier I get.' In other words, there's no such thing as luck, it's a combination of hard work and more hard work. With patience you'll start to see the opportunities that your hard work is uncovering. In time you'll see that, like Goldwyn before you, people will start to say you've been lucky and you can reveal your key secret: it's all down to hard work.

The first step in creating your own opportunities is to state clearly what you want to happen. Some people find this works best if they write it down; others say it aloud to the universe. It doesn't really matter, you can howl it to the full moon on a windy moor if the mood takes you. The important part is that you clearly say to yourself what it is that you're trying to do. A management consultant would say that this is objective setting, a sportsman would say this was visualising your goals. What has been shown time and time again though is that without a clear idea of exactly where you want to end up, it's extremely unlikely you'll ever get there. So, say aloud, precisely what the opportunity you want to create is.

I find visualisation to be very useful for me. What I like to do when I'm planning my aims is to pick an image that I can see happening at the end of the process. Whether it's stepping onto a podium, or getting a cheque, whatever it relates to. I then just work to make that image happen. I know what it is and I just have to bring it into reality!

Susie

Let's stick with the idea of a destination for the second step. If you've already stated aloud where you want to go to, the next thing you'd do for an ordinary journey is to go to Google Maps and work out how to get there. This would include looking at the various different routes you could take to reach your destination, looking at the pros and cons of each different route and choosing one to try first. This is exactly the same process you'll use to create your own opportunities. You'll research all of the different routes that people have taken to make something happen, look for your own routes and then plan which one is best for you to try first.

The key to success at this stage is to make sure that you keep your options open. You give yourself a huge advantage if you do not start closing off routes because of assumptions or inflexible attitudes. In the case of a journey this could be that you're adamant you want to drive to your destination, but look how many more options open up if you can take the train, or abseil, or fly! Keep an open mind at all times – you'd be amazed at how many people allow assumptions to keep them to a very limited number of paths in life. Your mind and approach must always be flexible if you're to master the skill of creating your own opportunities.

The final step is about resolution. You have stated your objective, you have a number of different ways you can reach that destination and you are about to set off. This is the point where you should allow your determination to crystallise in your soul. There are countless examples in history where the world has gathered to watch someone fail, only to see them achieve something incredible against all the odds. You can do that as well. It's a question of having resolve. Resolve is about every time you get smacked in the face, every time you fall over, every time you build a house of cards only to have it knocked over by a gust of wind, you will just laugh and get stronger. The laughing is important because having bad things happen to you isn't much fun and you can quite quickly go insane unless you let yourself laugh first. Once you've had a good chuckle about the latest setback: grow. Reach back into your soul and feel that the crystal has got bigger, your determination is twice the size, your ability to cope is magnified.

Fortunately, you will succeed. We know this because 10,000 setbacks cannot stop you, because the 10,001st time you will be there trying again. And that's how opportunities are created, of any kind. Use that process, get better at it and you'll see that creating opportunities for yourself – incredible things that the world will gather to see you fail at – are actually quite easy.

ACTION

Practise the steps of making things happen for yourself. Start with something small if it makes it easier but work through each stage and learn to use the process.

TIP

Ten great career habits to get into

1   Learn to shake hands properly. Practise introducing yourself. Smile nicely and make eye contact.

2   Always ask people for their business card (or contact details) and keep track of them. They are now part of your network.

3   Always be polite in writing and in speech.

4   Learn to remember people's names and their children's names. If you want to be really clever, remember one other thing about them.

5   Learn to stop talking, ask questions and listen to the answers. Solving other people's problems is a great way of getting them to solve yours.

6   Be honest. Cheating might seem like a shortcut, but try it and you'll discover the amount of energy that goes into guilt and the time and effort that you have to put into covering it up makes it easier to do it right the first time.

7   Help others.

8   Never stop learning. It doesn't have to be an official qualification, but never just rely on the one trick you mastered long ago.

9   Keep fit and be proud of your appearance. Stop short of vanity.

10 Routinely ask yourself if you are happy doing what you're doing, and if you're not make changes.

LESSON 2 – EVERYONE NEEDS TO KNOW HOW TO SELL (AND HOW TO BUY)

You have to practise selling and buying on a regular basis if you want to get really good at it, but the process begins by understanding how both skills work. Then it's simply a case of trying them over and over again. The reason that we don't often feel comfortable with buying and selling (and this is especially true of the British culture) is because it involves a) talking about money and b) a little bit of cheek. Neither come particularly easily, so it's only through going out and practising it in real situations that you'll ever become good at either. The thing to note is that if you can get good at these skills then you'll always be in demand.

There are many different styles of selling and you'll find which one you prefer the more you try it. There are countless books you can read if you want to learn about different sales techniques, but ultimately there's a fairly simple process that nearly all the techniques rely on.

○ **Know your product**. A salesperson needs to know their product inside out. They have to be the expert on it. The reason for this is that if a customer thinks that there are gaps in your knowledge then they'll wonder if any of the information that you are giving them is trustworthy. They know that you're asking them for money, and they'll be worried that you're just going to tell them what they want to hear. Truly knowing your product means that they can trust you. Above all things know your products' unique selling points (USPs). These are the virtues of your product that make it better than the other products out there.

○ **Know your customer**. You can (and should) do some of this research before you meet with the client. You should know as much as it is possible to know about them and their business. Doing this reassures your customer that you've taken the time to see how their business works. It also makes them feel good, as if they really matter to you – which of course they do. However, the other area of this that salespeople often don't understand is that knowing your customer also involves asking them lots of questions and listening to the answers they give.

○ **Explain how the product helps the customer**. From the first two points you have put yourself in a brilliant situation to explain clearly and simply how your product will benefit the customer. You should prioritise these benefits based on the questions you've asked and the issues that the customer has brought up. Don't just reel off the product's benefits – explain how it will solve the problems that the customer has mentioned.

○ **Answer the customer's questions**. This phase is also known as countering objections but really it's just about going back to listening to the customer. Finding out what information they need and giving it to them. Sales should always be a simple process. In many ways the different styles of sales mentioned above really start to differ at this point. Depending on whether you listen patiently to a customer at this point or railroad them into seeing your point of view is the dividing line between sales styles.

○ **Close**. The famous closing phase. This is where you wrap up the sale and ask for the customer's money. It's the bit many people find embarrassing. But if you've done your research for the first stages there should be nothing embarrassing about it. You've identified how your product – whether you're selling yourself to an interviewer, or a multinational business to an investment bank – answers the customer's needs. Then it's simply a case of reaching an agreement about the price. Before you go into the meeting you should know how much your product is worth and what you are willing to sell it for.

REAL LIFE

My favourite close is the assumption close – you assume that you've done your job right and you give them three options of product plans, you simply ask them which is best for them. Only in Britain do people have this fear of salespeople, in America they're super stars!

Tony

TIP ✓

Five rules for buying

1 Understand you're being sold to and agree to be a buyer only if it's something that you want.
2 Listen carefully to the product information. Ask questions to establish that you've understood the deal properly.
3 Understand the market – are there other products that can do this, why would you buy this particular one? If you need more time to research the market then do so.
4 Learn to resist the close. When someone is asking for an agreement it can feel rude to postpone, but learning to resist the handshake until you are happy is the key to being a powerful buyer.
5 Never, ever take the first price – always ask how they can improve the deal and what guarantees you have. Ask again how they can improve it.

LESSON 3 – FAILING IS FANTASTIC, GET BETTER AT IT

There are many things that are great about Britain. Chicken tikka masala, the Dyson vacuum cleaner and cricket to name but three. However, one of our most catastrophic drawbacks as a culture is our attitude towards failure. It seems remarkable that a country as small as ours which once had an empire that stretched around the world could have achieved as much as we have with this lousy attitude. For most people failure equals shame. We are embarrassed of failure. There are people out there, possibly including your parents, who have been so critically terri-fied of failing that they have spent their lives paralysed with fear. They've decided it's better to do nothing and not risk failing than try something different and maybe, only maybe mind, get it wrong. What do *you* think of that?

We sincerely hope that you think that it's ridiculous. Laughable. Crazy even. Hopefully, what you have read in this book will have helped you to see that trying different things, finding a range of paths to a destination, is a brave, wonderful and worthwhile thing to do. However, currently you exist in a system that has a fear of failure embedded in it. Your school is terrified of you failing, which is why they push you to do things that they believe are the best for you. Your parents have been worried about you failing from the day you were born, it's what parents do. Your friends have grown up in this culture too and so the only reaction that they know to have towards failure is to laugh at it, or pity it. Think of the phrase 'epic fail' and how often it crops up on the internet, and realise that you are part of a whole generation who have been trained to laugh at failure.

This in turn has made you one of them. You don't want to fail. You're desperate to avoid failure. Unfortunately, if you want to have a great life, if you want to achieve amazing things, if you want to be rich, if you want to fall in love or work on something that matters to you, it's almost certain that you'll have to embrace failure. You need to get comfy with failure. You need to understand that unless you are prepared to fall over and look stupid then you'll never do anything. Thomas J. Watson started IBM and he wanted to see failure all around him, because it meant that people were trying things that were difficult. 'If you want to increase your success rate, double your failure rate' was something he was quoted as having said, and it's true. All the good stuff is found out by doing things that are difficult, and in doing that you're going to fail. The brilliant thing is that failing doesn't hurt (OK, sometimes it hurts for a while) and it doesn't kill you (OK, it rarely kills you).

What failure gives you is a unique lesson. It tells you what you did wrong. As you rub your shin from falling off a skateboard, you very quickly realise what you did wrong and vow not to let that happen again. The more you fail, the faster the progress to the point where you do it right and land the trick. There's an urban myth that in America they don't consider you ready to start your own business unless you've been made bankrupt three times. Like many urban legends, it's nonsense – it's actually five times. That's right, unless you can prove that you've hit the bottom five times then you're not ready to succeed.

Enjoy that fact and make it part of your own approach to life. Once you've realised that failing isn't fatal, you begin to see the world as bulging with opportunities. Try to sympathise with all the people who wait on the sidelines for you to fail. They don't know any better and you now do. So what are you waiting for? Get out there, go and fail!

ACTION ⚡

This is a great exercise whenever you're starting something new. Spend half an hour imagining its failure. Set up the perfect storm of things going wrong and imagine exactly what would happen – what would people say? Who would be angry? Now work out what you would do in that circumstance, how you would get out of the situation and make it work. It's incredible how much sting that takes out of The Fear...

entry level opportunities for fresh talent

one of the UK's leading dairy companies we already supply a third of the nation's milk, but we've got big ambitions, so we're looking for equally ambitious new talent. It's an exciting time to join us. Throughout our sites the UK innovation and technology play vital roles, and with our talented people we are continually reviewing r processes and products to develop and grow. Take our plans for our new £150m dairy in Aylesbury, an portant part of our long-term growth strategy, it will be the world's first zero carbon milk processing facility – ilising the most advanced construction techniques and process technologies. We apply the same care and tention when it comes to our peoples' development too.

hether you join us in the technical and production team (these roles involve shift work), in a head office nction or on our apprenticeship scheme, Project EDEN, you'll benefit from some of the very best training ound. As you bring new ideas to help us become the world's most natural dairy, we'll offer you plenty of portunities for progression. We'll support and empower you to be your best. So for a great start to your career, merse yourself in our milk and dairy industry. To find out more, visit **www.arlafoodsjobs.co.uk**

Go on. Jump in.

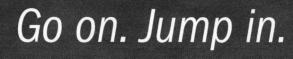

Closer to Nature™

Qualifications for a competitive advantage

> *CILEx is open to all. Qualifying as a lawyer via the CILEx route is cheaper & flexible*

Earn and learn at the same time with our unique route to becoming a lawyer, which doesn't need a law degree.

The qualifications cost from £4,500 to £7,000 in total, which is by far the cheapest way to train to be a lawyer. This covers all exam and study fees, and is spread over your study period (usually two years if full-time, or four years if part-time).

Our courses are offered at 70 centres and colleges across England or Wales, or by distance learning, so you can study at a pace to suit you.

And when you become a Chartered Legal Executive lawyer you can expect to earn £45,000 on average (some earn over £100,000). You can also be a partner in a law firm, represent your clients in open court, or even be a judge.

Over 92,500 people have chosen us for their qualification. Why not join them?

The only way to become lawyer without a university degree

Call **01234 845777** Email **membership@cilex.org.uk** Visit **www.cilexcareers.org.uk**

PROPERTY OF MERTHYR
TYDFIL PUBLIC LIBRARIES

CHAPTER NINE

THE QUALIFICATIONS THAT CAN DO MORE FOR YOUR CAREER THAN A DEGREE

This chapter in brief

- If you look away from the major qualification routes there are a number of skills well worth getting.

- As degrees and vocational qualifications become more commonplace, employers are looking for students to show something extra.

- These extra qualifications can also open up the rest of the world to you!

- They can also earn you more money. Lots more money.

It's great when you're in on a secret, not so nice when you're excluded. This chapter is all about giving you pointers about some of the qualifications and skills that exist which are considerably cheaper (and often free) to get than a degree and yet could help develop your career almost as much. If you're wondering why such a thing exists and why you haven't heard about it before, then you need to speak to the people who are responsible for the curriculum – there's no doubting that employers are keen to meet potential employees with these skills and qualifications.

PROFESSIONAL QUALIFICATIONS

So you've decided that you want to be an X. Rather than carrying on writing X, let's pick any career you can think to mention – such as an accountant. One route into accountancy is to go to university and study to be an accountant. However, you could also leave school and do everything you can to find work in an accountancy firm. You might have to start with a relatively low-level job, such as a data entry clerk, but you might find that various accountancy firms also have school-leaver recruitment programmes. You might be worried though that you've not actually learned how to do the job – this is where professional qualifications come in.

In most industries there is a professional body that represents the industry, promotes the occupation and provides training so that the industry has members that are well trained and a credit to their occupation. You'll find that professional bodies exist in most occupations. Most of these professional bodies have a training route that means you qualify as one of their chartered members, so basically you get the badge saying that the industry body has accepted you as a trained member.

REAL LIFE

People should know that professional qualifications are actually useful! I think you spend so many years getting qualifications which just seem like the passport to do the next level, that it's weird when you start your professional qualifications and you find them making you better at your job. Earning more is great too!

Karen

In most cases this can bypass the need to go to university entirely as you'll find that the professional qualifications are often the ones that employers want you to have. They want you to have a degree to get into the business in the first place, but they want you to do the professional qualifications to really specialise your training in that particular job. In many cases for university graduates, this means they start working in an area, only to find that they have to do more study. To be absolutely fair, a relevant university course will often mean you can skip some of the professional qualification exams, but you'll still have to do some.

Back to our example, if you wanted to be an accountant – you work in the accountancy firm, study with the chartered institute or professional body that best represents your career choice and usually your company will pay for the courses – because it means that you're becoming a better employee for them. No debt, qualifications that you can take with you from one job to another and an almost guaranteed pay rise when you complete them.

One of the biggest shocks for many school leavers relates to the various careers that allow this sort of training path. You've probably always thought that you'd need to go to university to become a lawyer, haven't you? Not true – take a look at the Chartered Institute of Legal Executives (ILEX). Think you need a degree to become a journalist? Not a bit of it – take a look at how many job adverts with news organisations mainly ask you to have the National Council for the Training of Journalists (NCTJ) qualification – that's not a degree, that's a professional qualification.

If you want to see if the career you're excited about joining has a professional qualification then the best people to approach are either the contacts that you developed in your career research or the professional body itself. You'll find that for some of the careers you might need a degree to get onto the course, but for many more you'll be surprised to see that relevant work experience is just as valid for entry onto the professional qualification.

ACTION

Look for the professional qualifications that exist for your chosen career. See how far they go and start looking at what you need to do for each different level.

LANGUAGES

The number of young unemployed has been growing for the last decade. At this point in time there are more than a million young people who are unemployed. When you think of a million people, especially when you think of them as competitors for the same jobs that you're going for, it can be very daunting. The solution to this feeling is to constantly add to the skills and abilities that you have, so that when employers are filtering the candidates your CV is the one they keep.

Learning to speak another language might seem like a challenge but it can be great fun, and once achieved it means that you could even consider working abroad, which increases the number of labour markets you can search in – massively increasing the number of opportunities open to you. If you want further encouragement you should know that the average salary boost given to a career when you learn a new language is anything up to 20 per cent. Across the course of your career that could well represent hundreds of thousands of pounds. If you've made up your mind to learn a new language you might be wondering which one you should learn. First up, take a look at the following list showing the approximate number of people who speak different languages:

1   Mandarin Chinese (720 million)
2   English (480 million)
3   Spanish (320 million)
4   Russian (285 million)
5   French (265 million)
6   Hindi/Urdu (250 million)
7   Indonesian/Malay (230 million)
8   Arabic (221 million)
9   Portuguese (188 million)
10 Bengali (185 million)
11 Japanese (133 million)
12 German (109 million)

You might think that from there it's a simple case of picking the top three, which would give you the cool ability to communicate with 1.5 billion people – or around one out of every six people on the planet. That would be great, but then it might not be the best thing for your career. For instance, even though your ability to speak Mandarin might open up the vast employment areas of China – how do you know that they even have the sort of business that you're looking to work in? Potentially, visa restrictions might mean you would have to emigrate before you were allowed to practise law, for instance.

The best bet when choosing a new language to learn is to look at the sorts of labour markets that different countries have. For instance, a huge proportion of China's economy is based on manufacturing. If this isn't something that you're interested in then potentially you should look at another language. Spanish would open up Spain and vast areas of South America, but these areas are lagging behind when it comes to the technology sectors, so if you wanted to work in IT they might not be right for you. There is currently, a huge demand for Arabic speakers in different areas such as journalism and security, so research how a language could help you progress.

Incidentally, don't just restrict your choice of language to exclusively spoken languages. Currently, the most in-demand languages in the world are computer languages. If you can speak to machines then there's nearly always going to be very well-paid work for you. HTML, Python, C++, XML, RubyonRails, all of these are worth investigating. Although they might look like gobbledegook to a beginner it's amazing how pleasingly logical a lot of the computer languages are, which is encouraging for any learner.

REAL LIFE

These days it's less about learning the hard core computer programming skills, but it's incredible how far you can get and what you can achieve by becoming very familiar and competent at different web building platforms like WordPress, Joomla and Drupal. If you could also edit photos and video then you're instantly employable. Learn how to sell and you could go self-employed.

Simon

EMPLOYABILITY SKILLS

Employability skills are perhaps better described as attributes. They're not things that you could necessarily get a certificate for (although increasingly colleges and universities are seeking to equip students with some kind of Employability Certificate), but they're the characteristics that genuinely drive employers wild with excitement. It's well worth spending some time looking at how you could prove to an employer that you have these attributes.

Communication skills

If an employer asked you how you could prove that you have good communication skills, what would you say? If you were stuck for an answer then you might automatically prove that your communication wasn't up to much! The sorts of things that make a great impression on employers are situations where you've had to excel at communication. Think about if you could show examples of the following:

O Presentations
O Acting or performing classes or shows that you've done
O Complicated written assignments
O Situations where you've had to display great diplomacy
O Communication under pressure – where you've had to convince someone.

Technical skills

The modern workplace is awash with technology. As part of a younger generation it's assumed that you will have an advantage when it comes to the use of technology because the computer was in widespread use when you were born. Bear in mind that this isn't the case for all employees! Again, think about how you would prove your excellence with:

O computers
O phones
O other workplace equipment such as printers or photocopiers.

This is one of the few employability areas where you could easily find a course that would give you a certificate that would prove you've attained a certain level of competence. The European Computer Driving Licence is one course, but others include Google and Microsoft certificates.

Flexibility

There's no getting around the fact that employers are a curious bunch at times. They say that they're looking for evidence of people using their initiative (which might also be described as being entrepreneurial, or working on their own) but then they also want you to show how you can work in a team. In many cases these two skills are at odds with each other. People either lead or are led, but it's useful to think about how you could show you can do both:

O When have you taken charge of a situation or group?
O Have you been a team captain? Did you organise a show? Were you voted bossiest member of your school year?
O What have you achieved as part of a group? Societies can be a good way of showing this, whether you sing with a choir, or do synchronised swimming – there must be something that you've done that can show how you work well with others.

Maddison Grant

After finishing her A-levels, Maddison Grant didn't want to face the stress of having large amounts of university debt. She felt nervous about making a big financial commitment given the current economic climate

I studied law, critical thinking, psychology and accountancy for A-Levels but my main interest was mathematics and problem solving. I found out about AAT whilst still at school. It was exactly what I needed in order to get a recognisable qualification whilst earning a salary.

'Studying AAT helped me find a job working in Credit Control for O'Neill Wetsuits and my employer now financially supports me in my studies. One of the best things about the qualification is that it's extremely flexible and allows me to study at my own pace.

'Choosing AAT over university was the best decision I've ever made. I've avoided debt, gained a recognised qualification and am gaining first-hand experience in my career of choice. I feel as though I am already a step ahead of everybody else who chose to complete a university degree.'

Maddison is on track to gain an internationally recognised qualification with AAT. With youth unemployment statistics over the million mark and graduate employment rates on the decline, the AAT qualification offers students the opportunity to combine study and work whilst gaining experience in a professional office environment.

Visit www.aat.org.uk for more information on how to get started or call our student recruitment team on 0845 863 0802. Get a step ahead of the rest with AAT.

Creativity

This is also sometimes referred to as problem solving. No employer is really going to be interested in the fact that you can play nearly all of Bon Iver's songs on the guitar. What they want to know is that when you're given some work to do that you're not constantly going to be asking how you do it. The sort of evidence you want to gather for this includes the following:

○ Problem solving – when did a problem occur that you had to sort out?
○ When have you shown a flash of genius?
○ What was your innovation that solved a problem?
○ When everyone was looking at a problem one way, why or how did you come up with a different way of looking at it?

Finances

It's sometimes forgotten but businesses are about making money. Companies are going to want you to demonstrate what's sometimes called commercial awareness. On one level this means that you know how to treat a customer (they're the ones who are always right, remember?), but it extends from there to the fact that you can count and add and subtract enough to run a till. At the top of it all is the fact that your business wants to make more money. If you can help them do that then you're going to get them excited about you:

○ When did you run a till?
○ When were you trusted with money?
○ When have you been in a customer-facing environment? How can you prove you were great at it?
○ How would you demonstrate some knowledge of the environment the business works in? Who are their competitors?
○ What is innovative and cool about their products?

TECHNOLOGY QUALIFICATIONS

We live in a digital world and as a member of the younger generation, it will automatically be assumed that you have a working knowledge of not just the essential word processing and finance suite of products, but that you can also navigate your way profitably around the social networking worlds. In many cases these are possibly things that you've grown up with, but not every school or college leaver is a computer whizz. That's why you should consider doing some work on the technology basics listed below. If you enjoy it you might also like to consider taking some of the more advanced skills listed below.

Technology basics

O Familiar (i.e. can open and do all basic tasks) with a word processor and spreadsheet (the most common packages are Word and Excel).

O Make a basic presentation with PowerPoint.

O Print something out.

O Access information and add an entry into a calendar program (Google Calendar or Outlook).

O Send an email (with and without an attachment).

O Open an attachment from an email.

O Understand the basics to backing up information and have a reasonable system for backing up all of your own information (e.g. using Dropbox or similar).

O Use advanced search techniques for Google and other search engines.

O Open a profile in a social network.

O Understand how to add an update to Facebook and Twitter.

O Show an understanding of the importance of information privacy.

O Add a video to YouTube.

O Take a screen capture.

REAL LIFE

There's an 'accepted wisdom' that women are worse with computers than men. In my experience it's not that the female employees are worse at computers, it's that they're a lot less confident. There's really no excuse for not having a basic computer literacy though, so whether you're a boy or girl brush up on your core skills before starting a job.

Toby

Technology advanced

- Advanced techniques with Word and Excel – e.g. mail merge and creating a number of different graphs and charts.
- Understand how to create and add information to databases.
- Create a presentation incorporating video and graphics.
- Resize and do basic corrections to images.
- Create a web page.
- Understand the basics behind search engine optimisation and how to do it.
- Edit a video and upload it to YouTube.
- Demonstrate a good awareness of the different hardware issues that can arise with a normal personal computer.
- Use computer anti-virus software.
- Understand the basics of a computer network.

There are any number of computer qualifications that you can get, which will all massively improve your ability to convince an employer that you are computer literate. As well as computing degrees there are qualifications in individual computer companies' products – which are often available for free. You can get short courses on Google's products for free. Microsoft certification will cost, but opens up a very well-paid area of technical support work. Finally, learning computer languages can enable you to achieve anything from designing your own Flash-based websites or program the sort of applications that make millions on iPhones and Android-enabled mobile phones.

ACTION ⚡

Cross off the skills you already have on the two technology lists above. Make a list of which items you have yet to get to and plan when you could address these skills.

25 SKILLS THAT MIGHT NOT EARN YOU ANYTHING BUT THAT WILL BE GOOD TO HAVE

1   How to manage your time.
2   How to cook a range of basic meals.
3   How to defuse an argument and avoid a fight.
4   How to clean and mow a lawn (including correctly loading dishwashers and washing machines).
5   Understanding basic home economics (creating meal plans, shopping, household budgeting).
6   How to look good in a photograph or video.
7   How to take good notes.
8   How to type.
9   How to do basic DIY.
10 How to tell if someone is lying to you.
11 How to end a relationship that isn't working.
12 How to choose what to wear.

13 How to stay safe in cities.

14 How to set and remember a secure password.

15 How to do basic car maintenance.

16 How to win an argument.

17 How to stand up for your rights.

18 How to start a fire.

19 How to use statistics properly.

20 How to manage your finances.

21 How to do basic first aid, including CPR.

22 Understanding how the political system in the UK works.

23 Understanding the basic principles of other cultures and religions.

24 How to be a good friend.

25 How to play several card games.

Competitive salary **+** In-demand skills **+** Work in any industry **=** Accountancy. It all adds up

Train to be an accounting technician with AAT.

Studying for the AAT Accounting Qualification through an apprenticeship is the smart way to get valuable work experience while gaining a widely-recognised professional qualification.

Not only will you earn while you learn, but you'll launch your career in finance in less time than a graduate – and with no debt.

Just like Shelley, you'll find lots of opportunities to land that first job. Leading companies such as P&G and BT offer AAT apprenticeship schemes. And you'll have plenty of options for further qualifications with fast-track schemes for chartered accountancy.

"The AAT qualification is the best choice I have made for my career and future aspirations."

Shelley Johns AAT student member
Jonathan Vowles Chartered Accountants

Think about a career in accounting. For a free guide to AAT, call us on **0845 863 0802** or visit **aat.org.uk/accountancy**

aat The professional body for accounting technicians

AAT is a registered charity. No. 1050724

HOW TO BEAT THE MOST COMMON PROBLEMS FACED BY SCHOOL LEAVERS

So you're about to leave school – all you've got to worry about is the graduation party and a bright new future, right? Well, kinda. We don't want to rain on anyone's parade, so let's keep this upbeat and say that now you've left school you're going to face an array of challenges that you might not have come up against before. Fortunately, your old pals at Not Going To Uni have put together a quick fix for some of the most common post-school problems.

1. FEELING LEFT BEHIND

There's an annoying thing you'll find about other people. It's that they don't readily express all the fears and worries that are going through their heads. So when you check their Facebook/Twitter profiles or just catch up in real life, it always *seems* as if they're not struggling with the same doubts and worries that you feel. The key to understanding this is that little word 'seems'. Everyone you know is just two bad days away from chaos. That's life. That's people. So now you know the secret you can be just as confident as the others because you know that it's really just pretend. Funnily enough, when you pretend you're confident it often works that you become confident. Try it out.

2. NO MONEY

There's a school of thought that mo' money equals mo' problems. At Not Going To Uni we prefer our grammar to be more conventional than that though, and we know that more money would actually be kind of nice. Regardless of why you want it there's no denying that money makes doing things easier. If you've got no money and you want to do something then it falls back to you to think of a way around it – and we'll make you this solid gold promise: there is always a way around it.

Let's take travelling. If you're desperate to do a gap year but can't afford it, how on earth can you go? How about volunteering? There are some schemes that pay your travel and accommodation costs in return for your work. Or how about going abroad to work? You can pay your airfare to Australia by fruit-picking when you're out there. Can't afford uni? How about looking into sponsored degrees? Trust us: there is always a way around it.

3. 'I DON'T KNOW WHAT I WANT TO DO!'

Great! Then you have reached a critical point in solving this problem. The first step is having a tantrum and throwing stuff around as you accept Step 1 – you realise you need to do some research. Step 2 is doing some research. Step 3 is living happily ever after. So how do you do Step 2? Go and see a careers advisor (a good one), start a list, do some work experience, talk to people, work shadow people, volunteer, travel. Do all of those things and realise what you like and what you don't. Maybe give yourself a set period to go and try five different careers or lifestyles you like the sound of. Then come back, compare your research notes and maybe make a more long-term decision. You'll make loads of mistakes, so don't worry about getting things wrong, it's inevitable. But if you're trying and learning you're always on the path to getting over that initial tantrum and finding out what it is that you want to do.

4. 'MY PARENTS DON'T SUPPORT ME'

In all likelihood that's probably not true. If they follow the standard parent format they love you massively and they think they know how to live your life better than you. That's their job, it's hard for them when they've spent 16+ years looking after you and caring for you. There's probably some rule of biology that once you've cleaned poo off someone else you're never going to be able to fully accept they are their own person. It's your job to prove them wrong, to show them that you can be trusted to make your own decisions – even if they're the wrong ones. So, instead of arguing (which is always going to convince them that you're just a brat who can't be trusted to make their own decision) talk to them. Put together a presentation. Explain to them why you're making your decision. Explain how you've looked at all the options and why this one appeals to you more than any of the others. You will get more respect and buy-in from your folks if you take this method. You might even get their full, unadorned support, but if you don't, take that on the chin and just ask that they accept your decision.

5. 'I DON'T KNOW HOW TO BECOME A...'

That's an easy one. Name any career you fancy and there will be a blue-print of how to do it on the web. Prospects (www.prospects.ac.uk) has a series of great careers profiles that you can follow for graduate jobs (but there's plenty you don't need to be a graduate to get). The other thing you can do is simply to steal other people's career paths. Find someone who does what you would love to do, find out how they got there and just copy it.

6. 'I'VE MADE THE WRONG CHOICE'

Good. Then you've already decided something. The key to solving this is to waste as little time as possible in sorting it out. We all make mistakes and start off down the wrong path sometimes, but the sooner you realise it and do something about it the less impact it actually has. Never, never, never, never, never, never, never carry on with something you don't want to do. Never.

7. GETTING FAT AND UNHEALTHY

It might seem like a funny one to mention but it's something that affects quite a few school leavers. This might be because while they live at home someone else looks after their nutrition, and when they leave home they sometimes don't have the dietary smarts to avoid it. They might also be celebrating their new-found freedom with rather too much junk food and booze. Keeping healthy is vital for success and happiness, so make sure you keep an eye on your weight and fitness. If you start putting on weight, do something about it. Ignore it and it will become a problem that will hold you back.

8. 'I'M SCARED'

That's probably very sensible. Doing something for the first time (like going away from home, or starting a new job) is completely different and challenges us. Fear is really just the body's way of saying to pay attention, which is useful in these new situations. Don't let it get out of control though. Channel it into excitement if you can and if you get too nervous then talk to someone about it. You'll be surprised how sympathetic people can be and there are always resources open to support you – friends, family, even Not Going To Uni.

9. 'I CAN'T GET A JOB'

See Chapter 7 on finding work. Often the key to getting around this is to try new methods. Don't just keep looking in the paper and being disappointed that your dream job hasn't appeared. Get out there and find it. Or get out there and create it.

10. 'I MISS SCHOOL'

You've just spent a couple of decades learning to hate the teachers and all that boring learning and now you've been out for less than a few months and you already miss it. Well don't worry, it's a feeling that many share. When you go from something so familiar to something different then it can lead to feelings of fear and a lack of confidence. If you're feeling this way then you need to start getting excited about the future. You might not have a fully planned out future that is driving you wild with excitement, so get those plans in place and you'll soon find that moving on is easier than you think.

MY SPECIFIC SKILLS LIST:

1 ....
2 ....
3 ....
4 ....
5 ....
6 ....
7 ....
8 ....
9 ....
10 ....

MY GENERAL SKILLS (TAKEN FROM THE CBI/NUS WORKING TOWARDS YOUR FUTURE REPORT)

Skill	Put these in order from 1 to 8
Self-management – your readiness to accept responsibility, flexibility, resilience, self-starting, appropriate assertiveness, time management, readiness to improve your own performance based on feedback and reflective learning	
Team-working – respecting others, co-operating, negotiating, persuading, contributing to discussions, your awareness of interdependence with others	

Skill	Put these in order from 1 to 8

Problem solving – analysing facts and circumstances to determine the cause of a problem and identifying and selecting appropriate solutions

Application of IT – basic IT skills, including familiarity with commonly used programs

Communication – your application of literacy, ability to produce clear, structured written work and oral literacy, including listening and questioning skills

Application of numeracy – manipulation of numbers, general mathematical awareness and its application in practical contexts (e.g. estimating, applying formulae and spotting likely rogue figures)

Positive attitude – a positive attitude encapsulates characteristics such as a willingness to take part and openness to new activities and ideas

Business and customer awareness – your basic understanding of the key drivers for business success and the importance of providing customer satisfaction and building customer loyalty

MOTIVATIONS (FROM STEVEN REISS, WHO AM I? THE 16 BASIC DESIRES THAT MOTIVATE OUR ACTION AND DEFINE OUR PERSONALITIES)

Pick three of these different motivations that are really drivers for your life and three that aren't.

○ **Acceptance**, the need for approval
○ **Curiosity**, the need to learn
○ **Eating**, the need for food
○ **Family**, the need to raise children
○ **Honour**, the need to be loyal to the traditional values of ones clan/ ethnic group
○ **Idealism**, the need for social justice
○ **Independence**, the need for individuality
○ **Order**, the need for organised, stable, predictable environments
○ **Physical activity**, the need for exercise
○ **Power**, the need for influence of will
○ **Romance**, the need for sex
○ **Saving**, the need to collect
○ **Social contact**, the need for friends (peer relationships)
○ **Social status**, the need for social standing/importance
○ **Tranquillity**, the need to be safe
○ **Vengeance**, the need to strike back/to win.

PASSIONS – WHAT DO I LOVE?

Note down ten things that you are passionately wild about.

1 ....

2 ....

3 ....

4 ....

5 ....

6 ....

7 ....

8 ....

9 ....

10 ....

INFLUENCES

Name three sources of influence on your choice of career path — what is it that they want you to do?

1 ....

2 ....

3 ....

MY FUTURE PATHS LONGLIST

1 Something I love doing

....

2 Something I love doing

....

3 Something I love doing

....

4 Random choice

....

5 Random choice

....

6 Random choice

....

7 Random choice

....

8 Random choice

....

9 Suggested by specific skills

....

10 Suggested by specific skills

....

11 Suggested by specific skills

....

12 Suggested by specific skills

....

13 Suggested by motivation

....

14 Suggested by motivation

....

15 Suggested by motivation

....

16 Suggested by parents

....

17 Suggested by parents

....

18 Suggested by parents

....

19 Suggested by friends

....

20 Suggested by friends

....

MY FUTURE PATHS SHORTLIST

These are five jobs or careers I'm genuinely excited by:

1 ....

2 ....

3 ....

4 ....

5 ....

MY FINAL SELECTION

....

....

....

....

....

....

....

THE PERFECT R&D YEAR PLAN

....

....

....

....

....

....

....

MY BUSINESS IDEA

....

....

....

....

....

....

....

INDEX

Fashion Retail Academy

Your career in fashion retail starts here

Apply online now

If you're interested in...

Retail Business

Buying

Merchandising

Visual Merchandising

Styling

Store Management

Fashion Marketing & PR

Garment Construction

Graphic Design

We've got courses for YOU...

www.fashionretailacademy.ac.uk

Case Study

Liam Price - Assistant Merchandiser

"Attending The Fashion Retail Academy provided me with a firm footing in the retail industry. I enjoyed my year at the Academy and gained so much experience, met so many influential people and got a job at the end of it as a Merchandise Management Development Partner at John Lewis Plc! I learnt so much in one year that I was immediately able to use in my job."

Liam is now an Assistant Merchandiser in online brands at New Look.

Why study at the FRA?

Full-time, Short Courses and Apprenticeships are available at the FRA's modern facilities in the centre of the West End.

Learn in this inspirational environment and draw on the FRA's extensive fashion industry contacts and business networks.

You will gain all the skills and experience to make you "job ready" for an exciting career in the retail industry.

LIVE.LIFE

Opportunity
to be more than an employee
to be a partner.

STARBUCKS UNIVERSIT

Starbucks Apprenticeship
Barista Mastery and Customer Service

☑ Do you want to learn new skills?

☑ Earn while you build a retail career?

☑ Be part of an amazing team and have fun?

We are seeking optimistic candidates with lots of initiative, who are looking to gain a variety of transferable skills while building a retail management career.

Being an apprentice means doing a real job, getting paid while learning new skills and gaining qualifications in Barista Mastery and Customer Service.

"At a time of record youth unemployment, we're very pleased to play our part in helping committed young people acquire new skills and paid employment when it's most needed."

Kris Engskov, managing director of Starbucks UK and Ireland

"I have learnt so much and I already feel like a member of the family here."

Laura, Canary Wharf store, London

- The apprenticeship takes 12 months with guaranteed employment at the end
- Learning will mainly be instore, with some classroom and webinar sessions
- Your career doesn't have to stop with the Barista Apprenticeship, there's opportunity to progress to the supervisor role and higher level apprenticeships

"I have received amazing support during the programme and I would recommend it to anyone who wants to progress and learn whilst working."

Anthony, Victoria Station store, London

To find out more about Starbucks and apply to be an apprentice, go to **www.lovecoffeelovepeople.com**

Selection criteria apply. Apprenticeship positions are available at selected stores only.